Knots Untied

A closer look at some of the
Bible's more difficult matters

Dr. Charles R. Vogan Jr.

Scripture taken from the HOLY BIBLE, NEW INTERNATIONAL
VERSION, Copyright © 1973, 1978, 1984 International Bible Society.
Used by permission of Zondervan Bible Publishers.

ISBN 978-0-6151-3937-1

Ravenbrook Publishers

A subsidiary of
Shenandoah Bible Ministries

━━━━━ ℘ ━━━━━

www.shenbible.org

Contents

Introduction

The Bible is both a simple and a mysterious book. Some of its teachings are so plain that even an unbeliever can understand its point; but some things that it says even the most experienced Bible scholar can't crack open until after years of study and prayer.

There have been many issues in Biblical studies that have proved to be difficult and confusing, even after thousands of years of work. For most, this means that such issues weren't meant to be understood and it's best to leave them alone. For others, it only represents an opportunity for a springboard into new pet theories – with little regard as to whether they are correct.

But without some sort of foundation, a building will eventually crack. These Biblical issues have for too long gone without satisfying answers and it shows – both in our society at large, and within the walls of the Church. There must be someplace we can begin getting at the truth of difficult areas in the Bible, or why did God lay them out for us to ponder? Somewhere is the key to unlock the door; somewhere are the instructions for beginning to untie the knot …

So I present these findings on a few knotty issues in the Bible, hoping that they will dispel some of the fog that usually attends these difficult passages. My approach with such issues has always been to dig down deep enough until I feel something foundational, something rock-solid that I am familiar with and that I *know* is true. Then, like an archaeologist, build back up using only those materials at hand that obviously fit in the scheme of things, until I have an entire structure that makes sense. There a few holes still left here and there, to be sure, but still I see a new picture that, to me, is what was intended in the first place by the Author of Life.

These issues, when investigated deeply enough and carefully enough, yield surprisingly useful truths that make the effort worth the while. May the Lord reveal himself to you in his Word, even in those passages that have for long hid their meaning from you.

The Temptation of Christ

The Temptation of Christ

In Matthew 4 we have the story of the temptation of Christ. The Spirit led Jesus out into the wilderness to fast for forty days, and then Satan approached him with particularly tempting offers to reveal himself to the world.

The standard interpretation of this story is that Satan knew exactly who Jesus was, and he wanted Jesus to "come out of hiding," so to speak, and tell the world that he was the Son of God. Perhaps, we are told, if he was successful in getting Jesus to announce himself openly, he would have achieved some diabolical purpose of his. But that interpretation doesn't seem to make sense in several respects. For one thing, the temptations that Satan offered Jesus are amazingly bold offers to be making the Son of God. Satan had already had dealings with God in the past, and he always came out the loser. What purpose would Satan have in challenging God to be almighty and powerful? Why would he come before God with a temptation? He's not stupid; he knows who God is, and how God works, and that whatever God does will only be the undoing of Satan's kingdom. Why would he purposely put himself within range of his enemy?

Another problem with the standard interpretation is the last temptation that Satan makes. If Jesus was the Son of God, and Satan knew that, why would he offer the world to someone who already owns the world? It's true that Satan has power over the world; the Scripture says that he's the "ruler of the kingdom of the air." (Ephesians 2:2) He has all nations under his thumb, doing his will, and therefore he certainly has the authority to give power and wealth (at least the limited resources he has access to, by God's permission) to whomever he wishes. But can he hope to tempt the Creator with only part of the Creation, and a perverted part at that? What does he hope to achieve by offering the Son of God a portion of what he is already an heir to?

In light of these perplexing aspects to the story, it seems to me that we have to take a different direction if we want to understand what's going on here. We need to ask another question in order to open up the mystery: did Satan know who Jesus was?

Did Satan know who Jesus was?

Let's assume for the moment that Satan *didn't* know who Jesus was. Does the story make more sense in that light? Let's review the facts with that assumption in mind.

- *Jesus was a man* – Let's not forget that Jesus was a man. It may not be impressive to us; but to Satan, for God to be a man was beyond comprehension. Nothing like this had ever happened in the past, and God certainly didn't let everybody know ahead of time what his strategy would be in sending his Son as a man. It was a complete mystery to everyone. This was the thinking behind the act of Jesus setting aside his glory: in doing so, people at first glance would miss who he really was. Satan was no exception.

In a war, it's wise on the commander's part to withhold certain information before the battle. After all, he doesn't want his enemy to know all of his plans! The element of surprise is one of the most powerful weapons we can use to defeat the enemy. And when the Son of God came as a man, nobody would be expecting such a move and certainly nobody could foresee how that would affect the outcome of the battle. Satan was just as much in the dark about the key strategy of God as anybody else was. The fact that he's on the scene, however, probing into the event should be no surprise; what would be surprising, and very unlikely, is that he would have known immediately what was going on.

- *"If you are the Son of God ..."* – It's interesting that Satan worded it like this. If he knew that Jesus was really the Son of God, why would he be so careful and wary around his opponent? What he's doing in this encounter, however, is probing: he's exploring because *he doesn't know what he's up against yet*. He's bold because he is dealing with a man, not God himself (at least as far as he knows at this point). He challenges Jesus, he makes irreverent interpretations of Scripture, he obviously doesn't have any respect for God – all because he thinks he is dealing with *just* a man, not with God directly. He's used to dealing with men and he knows what will successfully tempt them. And he's using those same tactics here.

- *The announcement of the Son* – In order to understand what's happening in this account, it would help tremendously if we look at the immediate context. Up in the previous chapter, we have the story of God sending his Spirit down on Jesus during his baptism. Keep in mind that all through the first three chapters of Matthew, we've seen many examples of how Jesus set aside his glory – he purposely put aside every outward proof of his divinity, power, majesty, anything at all that would strike people that he was God. What he did take upon himself was every possible outward appearance of weakness, humanity, unimportance, the very opposite of what we would expect to see in God.

Then, when Jesus is in the process of identifying himself yet again with sinners (his baptism – remember John's protest that it wouldn't be appropriate for the Messiah to undergo such a ceremony!) God announces his Son to the world:

"This is my Son, whom I love; with him I am well pleased." (Matthew 3:17)

This is the clearest statement yet to the dark world about the real identity of Jesus. It was made in the hearing of those at the Jordan waiting to be baptized, but we can be certain that it rang through the dark corridors of Satan's realm. It was like a trumpet blast that woke up the devil, and sent him scurrying to check out this challenger to his realm.

It's not surprising, therefore, that Satan shows up to see for himself who this man is. Again, we need to remember that we read this story after the fact – we already know who Jesus is. Satan didn't; he was in the dark about this man, and he struggled to understand what the Gospels have since clearly spelled out for us in detail.

- *The mystery of the Gospel* – The Gospel is the good news of the arrival of the King to take control over his Kingdom. Jesus announced it himself:

   "The Kingdom of God is near. Repent and believe the good news!" (Mark 1:15)

   It's called a mystery, however, by Paul – because on the surface it doesn't look at all like a spiritual takeover from Heaven!

   In reading this, then, you will be able to understand my insight into the mystery of Christ, which was not made known to men in other generations as it has now been revealed by the Spirit to God's holy Apostles and prophets. (Ephesians 3:4-5)

Physically, it looked for all the world like a poor carpenter's son preaching morals and doing good deeds, challenging the religious authorities, and getting crucified for his efforts. The result was a band of fishermen and laborers spreading around a new religion to take its place alongside the other religions of the world.

The truth, however, is underneath the surface. This was God's strategy: to cover the spiritual with the physical. Those who have been given "eyes to see and ears to hear" (Matthew 13:16) would be able to understand the mystery. Faith penetrates the physical veil and sees the spiritual reality behind it, the truth about the Son of God. The people of the world, however, with their physical senses, would never be able to understand Jesus. To believers, Jesus was the Savior; to unbelievers, he was no more than a Jewish teacher.

Satan was running right into the brick wall of this mystery. We could say that it was Jesus' first test case. His strategy of setting aside his outward glory in order to take on a veil of humanity paid off when he met in battle his first and most formidable opponent; his true identity remained undetected.

- *Satan knew God very well* – We also have to keep in mind the fact that Satan knew God, in one respect, far better than we do. He's known God since the beginning, since his own creation. He has seen God in his glory, in his majesty and power. He has had personal experience of God's power and wisdom – unfortunately, he was on the wrong end of the stick when it happened. He has seen the myriad of angels around God's throne, and has heard the oracles and commands that were issued from the throne to control the entire universe. We have seen little or none of this about God; all of our information comes from eyewitnesses, from secondary sources, not from personal experience.

So when Satan meets someone who claims to be the Son of God, he is naturally incredulous. We easily believe the story because we haven't seen the supreme height that Jesus used to occupy; Satan couldn't believe it because he *does* know God's supremacy. He can't fathom that the Master of the Universe would come, or even *could* come, down to such a low level. Satan despises humankind; he can't fathom the idea that the Creator would willingly become one of his own lowly subjects. And to make it even more of a mind-boggling conundrum, would God willingly put himself under the power and access of his old enemy the devil – right in the middle of Satan's empire of darkness? It was too much for Satan to accept right away.

The reason that Satan even tried to tempt Jesus was because he really didn't believe the claim about Jesus. His knowledge of the Almighty made him believe it to be impossible that God could become man; so he was pretty brazen about approaching this man and settling the problem. His intentions, I believe, was to try this impostor and score another success against God's kingdom: another prophet succumbs to the devil's schemes, unable to resist the temptations of the flesh.

There's another aspect to this drama that we should be aware of. Other religions claim to know God, but all of their descriptions of him are so off the mark – that is, they contradict the Bible so badly – that they obviously aren't talking about the same God that Christians believe in. In fact, they are *lies* about God that Satan himself has been careful to spread and develop throughout most of humanity.

One aspect of many of those religions is that their gods are anthropomorphic – that is, they have a human form or human characteristics. It's been a tool in the devil's bag of tricks for thousands of years. For example, the Greeks believed in man-like gods who lived on Mt. Olympus, and they have many stories to tell about the sins and foibles of their gods. After all, the Jews religiously held to the doctrine of Deuteronomy 6:4 – "The LORD our God, the LORD, is one," and Exodus 20:4 – "You shall not make for yourself an idol in the form of anything in heaven above or on the earth beneath or in the waters below."

When Jesus appeared, therefore, supposedly as the Son of God in human form, Satan of course was incredulous. Such an idea was a handy tool of his own to confuse and mislead ignorant fools away from the true God! He himself, however, was too smart to fall for that old trick.

- *Nobody knew yet* – We forget that at this point of the story of Christ, almost nobody knew yet who he really was. He hasn't done any miracles yet that would be convincing proof of his nature and ministry. He hasn't even done any teaching, which we are told was proof enough for some to think he was the Son of David and a force to be reckoned with. All that has happened at this stage was that he was baptized, and God announced openly that this was his Son.

Later on in the ministry of Christ, the thought would dawn on all sorts of people that there was indeed something special about Jesus. Even the demons that possessed people would challenge him and plead for mercy from him. But all that would come after his teachings and miracles; the news would spread around like wildfire behind him, as he lived and worked among the people. Even Satan would eventually realize his mistake in not recognizing the Son of God at the beginning.

It should be no surprise, therefore, and it is certainly something we would expect, that Satan probes at the beginning because he *really doesn't know* who this man is.

- *The proof would be a miracle* – Notice what Satan tempts Jesus to do: he wants to see a miracle. The standard interpretations of this passage imply that a miracle would be a sin on Jesus' part – as if he should do without bread! Actually the Lord was hungry, and making bread would have been no sin on his part. Satan wasn't tempting him to take care of his hunger – he was trying to draw Jesus out into the open with the one thing that would prove his claim of being the Son of God.

  If Jesus really was the Son of God, then he would be able to do impossible things – things that only God can do. Ordinary men can't do miracles because they don't have that power over Creation that the Lord has. They can only work with the materials at hand; Satan knew that. It looked for all the world that Jesus was only a man, but if he could be talked into doing a miracle, then Satan would know immediately that Jesus really was the Son of God (inconceivable though it was to him) and he could take appropriate measures to deal with this new kind of threat to his kingdom.

- *The religious leaders had the same problem* – Later in Jesus' ministry, the same problem arose for the same reasons. The Sadducees and Pharisees were terribly offended at his teachings, his claim to be God's Son, his authority, and his awesome displays of power. The entire ministry of Christ seemed to say that the leaders were dealing with an extraordinary man here, someone whose claims to divinity may well be justified. That didn't fit into their world-view, however, and they came to him repeatedly to challenge his claims.

The thing they were most offended about was his claim to divinity. To a good Jew, that was an insult to the spiritual God. There is only *one* God; Deuteronomy 6:4 teaches this. They weren't about to accept a pagan idea that God would come as a man. Their strategy, legally, was to get Jesus to clearly say that he was the Son of God and then, by their Law, they would have enough of a case to execute him for blasphemy.

So, they tried to tempt him to show his hand. They took the same approach as their father the devil (see John 8:44) – they challenged Jesus to produce a miracle, on the spot, something that only God can do. They of course didn't think he was God, and they expected only a blasphemous claim (with no proof) that he was God's Son. But it's interesting to see that their approach is the same one that Satan used. They knew exactly how to find the answer to the mystery!

> "What miraculous sign then will you give that we may see it and believe you? What will you do?" (John 6:30)

> "He saved others; let him save himself if he is the Christ of God, the Chosen one." (Luke 23:35)

Even at his trial, the one charge that successfully stuck and convicted him was the idea that a mere man claimed to be the Son of God.

- *It takes faith* – Jesus put aside his glory, in other words all the outward signs of his majesty and divinity, for a reason. He and the Father wanted people to believe the truth about him not by what their physical senses told them, but through *faith*. Salvation is made up of spiritual treasures, not earthly ones; we need to get in touch with Heaven if we want help. So, Jesus was determined not to look like God on the outside. People have to see something more than that in him if they are going to believe in him.

Faith is a special spiritual skill that penetrates the outward physical appearances of this world. We all know that it's often misleading to go by appearances. The way this world works, appearances can be deceiving – something that our senses told us would be good often turns out to be destructive. We need to penetrate beyond the physical world and see the spiritual foundation that holds the world together, which guides it along God's eternal purposes. We weren't born with this ability, however; it comes from God as a gift. It's the spiritual vision needed to see God as he truly is, to see this world for what it really is, and to see ourselves and our real spiritual needs.

Faith is the key to understanding Jesus – but not everyone has that faith. When Jesus put off his glory, he made faith an absolute requirement if we're going to understand him! Without faith we will never see or know the truth about Jesus. We have proof of that by the various reactions that people had toward him in the Gospels. Those who had no faith were confused and offended by him; they never did understand who he was or what he came to do – which is why they never took advantage of what he could do for them. But those with faith were able to see the truth about him.

You are the Christ, the Son of the living God. (Matthew 16:16)

The centurion replied, "Lord, I do not deserve to have you come under my roof." (Matthew 8:8)

Now if it's a requirement that a person have faith in order to know the truth about Christ, we can safely say that Satan was totally in the dark about him at the beginning! Faced with a man, not yet acquainted with his teaching or miracle ministry, knowing his beginnings as a carpenter's son and a poor man in society, and going only on his own powers of observation and reason, of course Satan didn't penetrate the veil and see the Son of God. He couldn't; faith isn't something that is open to Satan. God would never give him that gift. He can only go by what he sees. He has seen God in his glory, and he can see this poor, hungry, self-proclaimed prophet. He sees nothing more than that, since he doesn't have the spiritual vision that faith gives.

Jesus led by the Spirit

We have to keep in mind what Jesus was doing – there was a reason that he put aside his glory. Such a thing would seem not only unthinkable to those who know God best, but unnecessary. Why would the Son of God, the heir of the universe, dispense with what rightfully belongs to him – especially when it would come in very useful in his ministry?

The reason is that there has to be a new beginning for man, and Jesus himself is going to pioneer the way for the rest of us. Instead of directing things from the throne in Heaven, he came to earth to start up, try out, and establish every step of the way between the old and new creations. Since the old (first) creation was ruined by sin, it must be destroyed and then resurrected to a new kind of life – a life of the Spirit, righteousness, and eternity. And in an astonishing strategic move that would make sure that this program will happen and succeed, Jesus came himself as a physical man – was destroyed (on the cross) – and was raised from the dead as a new man. In himself he laid the foundations for the eternal Church, the new Creation, to replace the old world.

So he set himself limits to live under. For example, he willingly submitted to the Law's demands. (Galatians 4:4) He also was determined to live as God expects every man to live – which means that he was filled with the Spirit and led by the Spirit. (Matthew 3:16) He wouldn't have had to submit to the Spirit's leading like this, since he technically is the Spirit's equal (being one of the Persons of the Trinity, just as the Spirit is). But as a man he *must* submit to the Spirit, to "fulfill all righteousness."

It's in this special role – the perfect man – that Jesus deals with the temptations of Satan. He could have easily dealt Satan a death blow if he wanted and ended the matter. But his mission was to successfully live as a child of God who pleases God with everything he does and says. So he resisted the temptation to rise to Satan's bait, hid his glory from Satan (so successfully that Satan couldn't discern his true nature), and answered the temptations properly as a Spirit-filled man.

This is the source of Satan's confusion. He knew God well enough that the least smell of divinity – doing a miracle, for instance – would have alerted him to the presence of God in Christ. But he didn't have any idea of the plan of salvation: that Jesus himself would become the perfect man and carve out the path to Heaven for the rest of us to follow. It's Christ's identity with us that Satan didn't anticipate.

So Jesus refuses to accept the enemy's challenge; he won't give Satan what he's probing for. Keeping in mind the confusion, the spiritual darkness in Satan's mind, and the deliberate hiding of Christ's glory for purposes mentioned above, what would naturally occur to Satan? What would he think after offering Jesus the opportunity of "glorifying" himself by doing a couple of miracles – especially things that he certainly had the right and authority to do, *if* his claims were true?

What he would naturally think is that Jesus *isn't* the Son of God. He couldn't do the miracles required (so Satan thought), and only offered up some lame excuses based on loyalty to God. Satan has heard that line before from well-meaning desert ascetics and would-be prophets. He didn't take the "strong arm" approach to temptation that Satan is used to seeing in the glorious, sin-hating God. So, the devil figured that he was an impostor – but a dangerous impostor, nonetheless. Anybody who would start out his life work with a sign from Heaven and the blessing of a prophet of John's stature could be a dangerous opponent if not immediately controlled. Thus his last offer to Jesus.

"All this I will give you," he said, "if you will bow down and worship me." (Matthew 4:9)

Seeing it from this angle, the last offer makes perfect sense. Notice that Satan doesn't start by saying "if you are the Son of God" as he did the other two temptations. By now he thinks that the claim is false. Plus, this offer fits only with the theory that he doesn't believe that Jesus is the Son of God. What, after all, would the real Son of God want with the part of the world that Satan controls when he is already Lord of all? But if Jesus was only a man, this offer would be a staggering proposal for launching into a world-wide effort that wouldn't be possible to achieve otherwise.

Later, Satan realizes the true situation

Later on in Jesus' ministry, Satan obviously has learned from his mistake – but too late. A good commander will hide his plans at the beginning of the battle; then when events unfold, the enemy finds himself at a terrible disadvantage and can never catch up – even though he gradually learns what those plans were.

He can only helplessly watch his army being destroyed. Satan labored under the same disadvantages.

For example, the demons knew who Jesus was and pleaded with him to spare them any torment. How did they know? The answer is simple: by then Christ's teachings and works had been revealed, made plain, and advertised all over the countryside. If news travels quickly in human circles, it no doubt travels almost instantly in spiritual circles. Satan would have lost no time alerting his servants to the presence of the enemy in their ranks!

Notice too that even though the forces of Satan came to realize Christ's true nature, he strictly forbade them to announce it.

> In the synagogue there was a man possessed by a demon, an evil spirit. He cried out at the top of his voice, "Ha! What do you want with us, Jesus of Nazareth? Have you come to destroy us? I know who you are – the Holy One of God!" "Be quiet!" Jesus said sternly. "Come out of him!" Then the demon threw the man down before them all and came out without injuring him. (Luke 4:33-35)

The reason was that he was determined that people see him through faith, not by sight. He will continue moving about "incognito," so to speak, hiding his glory yet doing the work his Father sent him to do. People would continue to be confused about him and not know exactly what to think of him. But to those who received the Spirit from the Father, he would be seen as the Christ. Those who follow him will do so only because they can see past the outward appearances; they have the gift of faith that rises above this world and comes into the spiritual world of God.

Proof of Satan's incredulity

There is another proof in the Bible that Satan really was in the dark about Jesus. In 1 John we are told about antichrist, the great archenemy of God who works to destroy the kingdom of God.

> This is how you can recognize the Spirit of God: Every spirit that acknowledges that Jesus Christ has come in the flesh is from God, but every spirit that does not acknowledge Jesus is not from God. This is the spirit of the antichrist, which you have heard is coming and even now is already in the world. (1 John 4:2-3)

Evidently Satan really can't fathom the root idea of the Gospel – that Jesus has come into the flesh to become the New Man, which is our only hope for salvation. He can't see how or why God would do such a demeaning thing. All his servants attack this very idea of the Christ; it's how we can tell who have been deceived by Satan. Because none of his servants can accept the idea, this is strong proof that Satan – in the story about Christ's temptations – was completely in the dark about who he was really dealing with. Evidently he knows now who Jesus is and what he has come to do, but he still can't fully grasp what God has done. The incarnation of Christ is a weapon that destroys the foundations of the enemy's kingdom.

The Temptation of Christ

Why a Jew cannot be a good Jew

Why a Jew cannot be a good Jew
or
What happened to the Jewish religion in 70 AD

Most religions in the world were formulated a long time ago. The founders of each religion decided on what kind of god they wanted to worship, and they created the rules and principles of that worship that have lasted until our present day. Buddhism, for example, is based on ancient teachings that, if followed today, enable a Buddhist to worship the same gods in the same way that his forefathers did.

The Jewish religion is different. They worshiped the true God. *God* found *them*, and *he* gave *them* the rules for worshiping him. They didn't discover or make up anything new. They were supposed to preserve God's rules for worship through the ages, as a testimony to the rest of the world about what God is really like.

Another thing that makes the Jews different from other religions is this: about 2000 years ago, God took away from them the heart of their faith and left them without a foundation. They lost it all, except for their Bibles. The Jew today cannot worship God in the same way that his forefathers did.

Whether people recognize it or not, this was a catastrophe. It should make every Jew give a lot of thought about the state of his soul. The power and meaning of the Jewish religion is bound up in what God took away from them. It's as if someone blew up Washington DC, destroyed the American Constitution and Declaration of Independence, eliminated the entire government, and transported a few survivors to the moon. After such a disaster, the only things left are a few memories and photos – and that doesn't put one's civilization back together!

27

What we want to do is look at what God took away from the Jews, why that is such a fatal blow to their religion, and point out the lesson that God wanted them to learn from this.

What did God take away from the Jews?

The Jews claim that they were victims of their pagan neighbors. Rome made demands that the Jews couldn't conscientiously agree to, and the Jews rebelled. According to the Jews, they were entirely within their rights to resist Rome's rule – the Romans were forcing their pagan practices onto a nation that belonged to God alone. So the Romans, in 70 AD, destroyed Jerusalem and the Temple, and scattered the Jews away from Palestine.

But let's think about this for a minute. We know that the Temple was God's own house, that the land was his gift to the Jews according to the Covenant promise, that the pure worship of God was integral to the life and safety of Israel. And we also know that God was bigger than any nation or king that tried to set themselves against the people of God. Wouldn't it be reasonable to assume, then, that when all this and more was entirely destroyed and *not brought back* that God had something to do with it? God would not allow something so essential to stop unless he wanted it to!

We have seen this before in the history of Israel. The Jews themselves were a sinful people, obstinate and rebellious. It sometimes became necessary to send a pagan nation against them to punish them for their sins and wake them up to the spiritually dangerous state they were in.

Arameans from the east and Philistines from the west have devoured Israel with open mouth. Yet for all this, his anger is not turned away, his hand is still upraised. But the people have not returned to him who struck them, nor have they sought the LORD Almighty. (Isaiah 9:12-13)

Woe to the Assyrian, the rod of my anger, in whose hand is the club of my wrath! I send him against a godless nation, I dispatch him against a people who anger me, to seize loot and snatch plunder, and to trample them down like mud in the streets. (Isaiah 10:5-6)

He warned the Israelites, as they were waiting just outside of Jericho before they had entered the Promised Land, that he would deal harshly with them if, in their new land, they rebelled against him and worshiped false gods. Their punishment would come at the hands of invading armies.

The LORD will bring a nation against you from far away, from the ends of the earth, like an eagle swooping down, a nation whose language you will not understand, a fierce-looking nation without respect for the old or pity for the young. They will devour the young of your livestock and the crops of your land until you are destroyed. They will leave you no grain, new wine or oil, nor any calves of your herds or lambs of your flocks until you are ruined. They will lay siege to all the cities throughout your land until the high fortified walls in which you trust fall down. They will besiege all the cities throughout the land the LORD your God is giving you. Because of the suffering that your enemy will inflict on you during the siege, you will eat the fruit of the womb, the flesh of the sons and daughters the LORD your God has given you. (Deuteronomy 28:49-53)

This happened many times in Israelite history. They were overrun by the Philistines, by the Moabites, by Egypt, by Assyria, by Babylon, by Greece, and finally by Rome. God sent prophets to them before each disaster, warning them to turn away from their sins or be punished, but they wouldn't listen. So God used the harshness of pagan armies to punish his people.

After each of these disasters, a remnant of the Jews managed to put their lives back together and get on with the business of worshiping God as they ought. The absolute longest they had to do without the essentials of their religion was during the 70 year Exile in Babylon. When that time was over, they returned under Ezra and Nehemiah and rebuilt the Temple and Jerusalem. But when the Romans destroyed Jerusalem in 70 AD, the Jews lost just about everything *and to this day haven't been able to get it back.* There is still a remnant of Jews, scattered around the world in other nations, but the old Israelite religion is no more.

For those who have eyes to see, this is the hand of God. He has taken their precious inheritance away from them and given it to the Gentiles. The Jews are left destitute; the very things that enabled them to approach God and have a relationship with him are gone. Like the picture of the Glory of God leaving Jerusalem in the prophet Ezekiel, the Lord has left the Jews (for the time being) and taken his household treasures with him.

> She named the boy Ichabod, saying, "The glory has departed from Israel" – because of the capture of the ark of God and the deaths of her father-in-law and her husband. She said, "The glory has departed from Israel, for the ark of God has been captured." (1 Samuel 4:21-22)

> Then the glory of the LORD departed from over the threshold of the temple and stopped above the cherubim. While I watched, the cherubim spread their wings and rose from the ground, and as they went, the wheels went with them. They stopped at the entrance to the east gate of the LORD's house, and the glory of the God of Israel was above them. (Ezekiel 10:18-19)

I'm not sure the Jews understand the terrible importance of this fact. *It's impossible for a Jew to be a good Jew without these treasures.* He cannot fulfill his calling without them; therefore he cannot relate to God – he is cut off from Heaven. It's like asking a race car driver to finish the race without his car, or like trying to talk to someone in another city without a telephone. It can't be done.

Actually this desperate state of affairs was first predicted by one of the Old Testament prophets.

> For the Israelites will live many days without king or prince, without sacrifice or sacred stones, without ephod or idol. Afterward the Israelites will return and seek the LORD their God and David their king. They will come trembling to the LORD and to his blessings in the last days. (Hosea 3:4-5)

It first happened with the Exile. The Jews lost everything that made them unique – so that they would turn away from their sin and worldliness and turn back to God. With the same lesson in view, God has once again destroyed the Jewish system so that they will come back to God on his terms now – not relying on that old physical system but looking for a better spiritual system.

Let's make a list of the things that God has removed from Israel.

- **The Temple** – the Temple was crucial to the life of Israel. *First*, the Temple was the house of God, the very dwelling of God among men. What a mercy that the infinite and otherwise unknowable God came down to earth to reveal himself – not only to show the Israelites who he was, but to remain accessible to them whenever they wanted to approach him. All they had to do was turn toward the Temple and call on his Name, and he would hear them.

May your eyes be open toward this temple day and night, this place of which you said you would put your Name there. May you hear the prayer your servant prays toward this place. (2 Chronicles 6:20)

Second, the Temple was the site of the sacrifices that the Law prescribed for their sins. Only the Israelites, among all nations, knew the true meaning of righteousness – and, therefore, what sin really was. They had the benefit of the Law's careful scrutiny of their souls, pointing out their sins that so offended a holy God. Once they learned what sin was, the Law gave them a way of taking care of that sin so that God wouldn't hold it against them. They could bring an animal to the Temple and put it to death for their sins, so that they wouldn't have to die. It was an awesome sight – all that blood and suffering and dying on the Temple grounds. But it made them grateful that this utterly holy God had provided a way of escape instead of demanding *their* punishment, as he does with other peoples.

Now if God would take the Temple away from them, where would they be? They would be without God and without hope! God would be gone. They wouldn't be able to approach him anymore; therefore their prayers would go unanswered. Their protection would be gone – so they would be easy prey for all their enemies to persecute.

What is worse, they would lose their privilege of a sacrificial atonement for their sins. They themselves would now have to bear the burden of their sins. They couldn't put their sins, and therefore their punishment, on another victim. Now they are open to the wrath of God, not his mercy. He will not heed their pleas for forgiveness, because according to the Law someone must die for sin – either the sinner himself or an innocent victim in his place.

This situation is catastrophic for the Jews. It means that they are now as helpless and open to the punishment of God as their pagan neighbors are, with absolutely no help available. The Temple was their refuge from the destroying angel, and now it's gone. It's as if a soldier has lost all his weapons and now he's facing the enemy helpless – death is sure and certain.

Right now the Temple Mount – the huge platform where the Jewish Temple once stood – is owned by the Muslims and is the site of several Muslim mosques, the most notable being the Dome of the Rock. The Jews aren't even allowed near the area.

Christians have a sacrifice that satisfies the Law in the death of Jesus. He was a perfect man, perfect and righteous by the Law's standards, sacrificed by God the Father for our sake. In his death we have forgiveness of our sins – once for all this time, for any who will come to him for forgiveness.

> Unlike the other high priests, he does not need to offer sacrifices day after day, first for his own sins, and then for the sins of the people. He sacrificed for their sins once for all when he offered himself. (Hebrews 7:27)

His blood was spilled on earth, but the altar before the throne of God in Heaven glistens with his blood as well. What it did was open the door to God's throne in Heaven. Now because of his sacrifice we can approach God with confidence and present our requests directly to him.

Therefore, brothers, since we have confidence to enter the Most Holy Place by the blood of Jesus, by a new and living way opened for us through the curtain, that is, his body, and since we have a great priest over the house of God, let us draw near to God with a sincere heart in full assurance of faith, having our hearts sprinkled to cleanse us from a guilty conscience and having our bodies washed with pure water. (Hebrews 10:19-22)

The whole point of the Law in the Old Testament was that the earthly Jewish system, imperfect as it was, pointed to this perfect ceremony that really does take away our sin and bring us back to our Creator in peace and righteousness.

The blood of goats and bulls and the ashes of a heifer sprinkled on those who are ceremonially unclean sanctify them so that they are outwardly clean. How much more, then, will the blood of Christ, who through the eternal Spirit offered himself unblemished to God, cleanse our consciences from acts that lead to death, so that we may serve the living God! (Hebrews 9:13-14)

And by means of God's Spirit living in us, we now have continual fellowship with God – God lives with us, and we with him. The root idea of the Temple, that it was the place where you could come meet with God, is permanently solved for us.

We proclaim to you what we have seen and heard, so that you also may have fellowship with us. And our fellowship is with the Father and with his Son, Jesus Christ. (1 John 1:3)

- **The Kingdom** – When Israel was a nation, they at least had the chance to obey the Law and take advantage of the Temple opportunities. But when the nation was destroyed and the Jews dispersed around the world, they lost that opportunity. Now they *can't* be the people of God as God intended for them.

The Law, or the Torah, is the first five books of Moses – Genesis, Exodus, Leviticus, Numbers, and Deuteronomy. Here is the heart of Judaism. The Lord gave the Israelites the Law to do for them as the Constitution does for the United States: it defines the nation; it lays the groundwork for their legal, social, political and religious life.

The Law consists of 613 commandments. Each of these commands links with others – it all forms a tight and meaningful system. Take any of these laws out of the picture, and the whole system collapses. That's why the Israelites were instructed to obey *all* the laws, not just some of them.

> The LORD commanded us to obey all these decrees and to fear the LORD our God, so that we might always prosper and be kept alive, as is the case today. And if we are careful to obey all this law before the LORD our God, as he has commanded us, that will be our righteousness. (Deutero-nomy 6:24-25)

So if you want to destroy the Jewish religion, simply remove any key ingredient from the Law – they are now helpless to follow the rest of it. This is exactly what happened when God removed the Temple and its system of sacrifices. In fact, he didn't just remove a key ingredient, he took the very heart and soul out of Judaism!

There are all kinds of things that the Jews can't do now. They still pride themselves on following the Law, but they aren't being honest with themselves when they claim that. For example, most people are familiar with their "kosher" laws – the requirements that their food be ceremonially clean, both in the source and preparation of the food. And it's true that the Law requires that they keep away from unclean food and even unclean utensils used for cooking. What they can't do anymore is *deal* with unclean food, people, and utensils! When something became unclean, there had to be a sacrifice or ceremony at the Temple to make it clean again. But the Temple is gone! There aren't any more sacrifices available. The Jews have themselves been unclean, and living in an unclean world, for the last 2000 years with no way to fix the situation.

Another problem involves living side by side with Gentiles who aren't living by the Law. What does one do when the Law requires all of God's people to rest on the Sabbath – but the electricity and heat and transportation facilities and food services and mail and a myriad of other details in our modern society continue to function on the Sabbath? The country we live in isn't going to enforce God's Law. How then can the Jews live in obedience to all of the Law when their neighbors make it impossible?

The typical response to this is that we simply have to do our best and follow the part of the Law that we are able to follow; we aren't responsible for the problems that others bring into the picture. But this handy solution doesn't satisfy the Law itself. God required perfect obedience, following *all* of the Law – "*that* will be our righteousness." Read the Law for yourself. Whenever someone was guilty of either breaking the Law, or not carrying it out, they were labeled sinners and either had to offer a sacrifice for their sin or die under the hand of the Law. There wasn't any room for latitude.

> Everyone who sins breaks the Law; in fact, sin is lawlessness. (1 John 3:4)

> For whoever keeps the whole Law and yet stumbles at just one point is guilty of breaking all of it. For he who said, "Do not commit adultery," also said, "Do not murder." If you do not commit adultery but do commit murder, you have become a lawbreaker. (James 2:10-11)

Anybody who claims to follow the Law is being foolish. Nobody keeps anywhere near the 613 commands of the Mosaic Law. Most people don't even know what many of those laws require! For example, here are a few of the commands that God gave his people to follow.

Restitution for sacrilege	*Leviticus 5:16; 22:14*
The fruits of fourth-year plantings	*Leviticus 19:24*
Peah for the poor	*Leviticus 19:10*
Defective grape-clusters for the poor	*Leviticus 19:10*
The first tithe	*Numbers 18:21, 24*
The second tithe	*Deuteronomy 14:22*
The Levites' tithe for the priests	*Numbers 18:26*
The poor man's tithe	*Deuteronomy 14:28*
The avowal of the Tithe	*Deuteronomy 26:13*
Recital on bringing the first-fruits	*Deuteronomy 26:5*
The dough-offering	*Numbers 15:20*
Renouncing as ownerless produce of the Sabbatical year	*Exodus 23:11*

Did you know about these laws? Is there anybody today who follows these laws strictly, as they are written? For instance, without the Temple, one can't follow the Tithe laws at all – the purpose of the Tithe was to make sure there was plenty of food in the Temple storehouses for the

37

pilgrims during the three annual feasts in Jerusalem. But none of that exists now. In fact, even the Jews don't observe anywhere near the majority of the Law's requirements.

The problem is that the Jews just don't want to face this impossible situation that they're in. Since the Jewish Kingdom is gone, nobody can truly enforce any of the Mosaic Law. We all know that the Law is strict. If, for example, the IRS demands that you turn over 10% of your income to the government as taxes, you aren't free to send them a truck full of apples instead, claiming that you don't have the cash on hand right now. They won't accept that! You had better find the money or you're going to court. So when God's Law demands that you do 613 things, you aren't free to dispense with some of those demands on the excuse that you can't do that or the society you live in won't allow such a thing. You must do it or be guilty of breaking the Law. That is the dangerous predicament that the Jews are in right now – they are obligated to keep the whole Law, but they can't.

Well, some of them would say, surely God will forgive us our omissions since we don't have the Temple available to us. But that's assuming that everything is all right legally between you and God! If, however, he took away the Temple as a punishment, then he is setting you up for destruction – you are sinning against him, you can't help but sin against him, and there is no way out.

Jesus has taken care of the Law's requirements for us, better than we could have done the job ourselves. He took on a human body just for this purpose – so that, finally, a man would obey the Law's commands perfectly, something that God has wanted to see since the beginning of time.

Therefore, when Christ came into the world, he said: "Sacrifice and offering you did not desire, but a body you prepared for me; with burnt offerings and sin offerings you were not pleased. Then I said, 'Here I am – it is written about me in the scroll – I have come to do your will, O God.'" (Hebrews 10:5-7)

Now, whoever comes to Christ for salvation and righteousness will be filled with his Spirit and made perfect, just as he is.

Therefore, there is now no condemnation for those who are in Christ Jesus, because through Christ Jesus the law of the Spirit of life set me free from the law of sin and death. For what the law was powerless to do in that it was weakened by the sinful nature, God did by sending his own Son in the likeness of sinful man to be a sin offering. And so he condemned sin in sinful man, in order that the righteous requirements of the law might be fully met in us, who do not live according to the sinful nature but according to the Spirit. (Romans 8:1-4)

He has restored the Kingdom of God – he himself is the King. And rather than run the risk of man messing up his Kingdom, Jesus will enforce *and observe* the Law for us.

Do not think that I have come to abolish the Law or the Prophets; I have not come to abolish them but to fulfill them. I tell you the truth, until heaven and earth disappear, not the smallest letter, not the least stroke of a pen, will by any means disappear from the Law until everything is accomplished. (Matthew 5:17-18)

- **Their Genealogies** – The Jews kept careful records of their family genealogies. The reason that they did this was because they had to prove their Jewishness if they wanted to enjoy the privileges of Jews. They had to show a direct line of descent from former Jews in good standing if they wanted the Covenant Promises.

If one of our ancestors died and left a large estate for the heirs, we would have to be able to prove in court that we are one of the legal descendants if we want to receive part of the inheritance. Without that proof, we would have no legal claim to the estate. People all around the world, in all sorts of cultures, deal with this same problem, and so they have various ways of keeping track of what their family line is.

In the Bible, the Jews' family genealogies extended further back than most other people bother to keep records for. Every one of them could trace their family back to Abraham himself! For instance, let's look at Moses' family record:

> These were the names of the sons of Levi according to their records: Gershon, Kohath and Merari. Levi lived 137 years. The sons of Gershon, by clans, were Libni and Shimei. The sons of Kohath were Amram, Izhar, Hebron and Uzziel. Kohath lived 133 years. The sons of Merari were Mahli and Mushi. These were the clans of Levi according to their records. Amram married his father's sister Jochebed, who bore him Aaron and Moses. Amram lived 137 years. (Exodus 6:16-20)

Levi was the son of Jacob, who was the son of Isaac, who was the promised son of Abraham — and so Moses had proof that he was directly descended from the heir of the covenant. Without this proof he would have no right to the promises of God.

The Law itself forbade anybody but a descendant of Aaron to act as a priest in the Temple. "This was to remind the Israelites that no one except a descendant of Aaron should come to burn incense before the Lord, or he would become like Korah and his followers." (Numbers 16:40) In order to serve the Lord in the Temple, a man had to prove that he was in the family line of Aaron. Some people who claimed to be in that family couldn't prove it! For example, when Ezra and the exiles returned from captivity in Babylon to Jerusalem, their job was to rebuild the city and the Temple and restore the worship of God as it had been before the exile. One of the first orders of business, therefore, was to find enough priests to begin the sacrifices in the Temple. Some of them, though, couldn't prove their ancestry:

> The following came up from the towns of Tel Melah, Tel Harsha, Kerub, Addon and Immer, but they could not show that their families were descended from Israel: The descendants of Delaiah, Tobiah and Nekoda 652. And from among the priests: The descendants of Hobaiah, Hakkoz and Barzillai (a man who had married a daughter of Barzillai the Gileadite and was called by that name). These searched for their family records, but they could not find them and so were excluded from the priesthood as unclean. The governor ordered them not to eat any of the most sacred food until there was a priest ministering with the Urim and Thummim. (Ezra 2:59-63)

Earlier, when the Israelites came out of Egypt and swept into the Promised Land, they divided up Canaan by tribes: each person belonged to a particular tribe, named after one of the original sons (or grandsons) of Jacob, and all the people in that tribe would live in the part of Canaan assigned to them. For example, the descendants of Judah lived in the area where Jerusalem is, and the descendants of Dan lived in the northernmost reaches of Palestine. It was obvious why a strict record of a person's family tree was important: they got part of the promised land if they could show that they were part of the family. In fact, there was one family who had only daughters — no sons — who nevertheless claimed part of the inheritance:

> Now Zelophehad son of Hepher, the son of Gilead, the son of Makir, the son of Manasseh, had no sons but only daughters, whose names were Mahlah, Noah, Hoglah, Milcah and Tirzah. They went to Eleazar the priest, Joshua son of Nun, and the leaders and said, "The Lord commanded Moses to give us an inheritance among our brothers." So Joshua gave them an inheritance along with the brothers of their father, according to the LORD's command. (Joshua 17:3-4)

There were certain elements that the Lord definitely didn't want in Jewish circles! The Moabites, for example – they caused a great deal of harm to the Israelites during their wandering in the desert. Genealogy in this case guarded the race against unwanted aliens.

> No Ammonite or Moabite or any of his descendants may enter the assembly of the LORD, even down to the tenth generation. (Deuteronomy 23:3)

The Law prevented other undesirables from entering the assembly of the righteous.

> No one born of a forbidden marriage nor any of his descendants may enter the assembly of the LORD, even down to the tenth generation. (Deuteronomy 23:2)

The only way to make sure that the Law would be obeyed in matters like these was to keep strict family records. Thus the importance of genealogy to the Jews.

In all these records of the Bible, you will notice, the Jew was careful to show his direct line of descent from Abraham. The promises were given directly to Abraham and through him to his descendants — never directly to anybody else.

> I will establish my covenant as an everlasting covenant between me and you and your descendants after you for the generations to come, to be your God and the God of your descendants after you. (Genesis 17:7)

The only way that someone could lay claim to those promises was to prove that they were children of Abraham. Everybody in Israel knew this, and that's why they kept such strict records of their families.

The Jews of today, however, have no genealogical records. Most of them are pretty sure, through family traditions, that they are Jewish, but they can't establish anything more than that. For all they know, a Gentile in the Middle Ages married into a Jewish family and became their ancestor! And certainly nobody knows now what tribe they came from. [1]

And if there are no records, then there can be no claims. This is a simple point of Law that any nation recognizes. One can't just march into court and demand the inheritance if he doesn't produce adequate documents proving his relationship to the deceased. And there is no way that God is going to relax this standard. He demands purity, holiness, and devotion from everyone. Only this kind of society will properly and truly glorify him. He won't allow a nation of mongrels descended from immoral wretches to carry his Name! That's exactly why, from the very beginning, he made promises only to the Jews and not to the pagan Gentiles – the genealogies kept out the undesirables.

Well, a Jew would say, can't we start over somewhere? Can't we make a general call to all Jews around the world and gather together a new nation of Jews in Israel, devoted to God? Wouldn't God bless us then? The problem with this, however, is that the Covenant was given to *Abraham* and *his descendants*. The Law in this case requires proof of an heir, not devotion. I suppose that a person could make claims of inheritance if he wants to, and try to force the issue, but it takes two to make this work. God will not go back on his sworn promise to Abraham and break his Covenant, and without documentation you cannot make your case in God's court that you're Abraham's heir.

We still see this practice of keeping strict family records in the life of Christ himself. At the beginning of the

---

[1] The Levites are the only ones who have a slight chance of being identified. It's possible that modern technology can pick out the DNA of the Levite (or priestly) line, something that scientists are working on now.

gospels of Matthew and Luke, we find the family tree of Jesus:

> A record of the genealogy of Jesus Christ the son of David, the son of Abraham. (Matthew 1:1)

> He was the son ... of Abraham ... the son of God. (Luke 3:23, 34, 38)

In Jesus there meet two powerful lines of descent: being the Son of God, he has all the treasures of Heaven available to him, and being the son of Abraham he is part of the people of God. He now picks up the mantle of the Heir of Abraham, assigned to carry the responsibility of the Covenant promises and the source of blessing for the entire family of Abraham. In Jesus you will find the fulfillment of all the promises made to Abraham and his children.

> The promises were spoken to Abraham and to his seed. The Scripture does not say "and to seeds," meaning many people, but "and to your seed," meaning one person, who is Christ. (Galatians 3:16)

And to prove that you have a right to the Covenant, all you have to do is prove that you're of the same family of Abraham – that you have the faith of your father Abraham.

> Abram believed the LORD, and he credited it to him as righteousness. (Genesis 15:6)

> Therefore, the promise comes by faith, so that it may be by grace and may be guaranteed to all Abraham's offspring – not only to those who are of

the Law but also to those who are of the faith of Abraham. He is the father of us all. (Romans 4:16)

You are all sons of God through faith in Christ Jesus, for all of you who were baptized into Christ have clothed yourselves with Christ. There is neither Jew nor Greek, slave nor free, male nor female, for you are all one in Christ Jesus. If you belong to Christ, then you are Abraham's seed, and heirs according to the promise. (Galatians 3:26-29)

• **The Covenant Promises** – The Promises of the Covenant with Abraham was a family treasure, passed down through the generations from father to son. Each Israelite who could prove his family genealogy could lay claim to the Promises.

The story begins in Genesis when God called Abraham from Ur of the Chaldees and sent him to Canaan to take possession of the land. The ceremony is recorded for us in Genesis 15. There the two of them made a "covenant" – which in that day consisted of cutting certain animals in two and laying the halves on the ground. Then each party would walk between the animal pieces and promise such and such to the other party – swearing to do it upon penalty of ending up like these animals if they didn't. It was a very sobering transaction and not entered into lightly.

The Lord promised four things to Abraham. *First*, he promised him a Son, an heir to inherit the family estate. That heir would be a "miracle baby," born to a woman who was way beyond child-bearing age. *Second*, he promised him the land of Canaan – which also would have to be a miracle, since at the time it was owned by Canaanites who had no intention of letting this alien take their land away from them. ***Third***, he promised that his descendants would become a great nation. This too was a thing not easily done, because there were a lot of ways in those days that a family line could come to an abrupt end. Besides, who would expect that one's descendants would be so numerous as to make an entire nation? ***Fourth***, God promised Abraham that he would be a blessing to all the nations on earth.

To any other person these promises would have been strange and mysterious, if not in what they meant then at least in how the Lord could bring them about. But to Abraham, they were a treasure; he saw in them his own salvation as well as the salvation of all of his children.

The heir – we've already looked at how important a genealogy would be for the Israelites. They had to prove their relationship to Abraham if they wanted anything from God. But with this proof they could boldly enter the Temple of God and ask for anything they wished, because God would not withhold anything good from his children.

The land – Canaan proved to be a source of rich blessing and pleasure to the people of God. They had ready-made homes to live in, already-plowed fields, fruit trees, wine and olives and figs – everything they could want and more in abundance. They had protection from their enemies there, living in the mountains. They built a beautiful capital city – Jerusalem – and (in times of peace) enjoyed the rich trade routes along the Mediterranean Sea as their neighbors traveled back and forth between Egypt and Mesopotamia.

The nation – God gave his people the Law, which was a precious treasure in itself. Through the Law he ruled over them in justice and righteousness. Through the Law the Israelites learned about the holy God and how to please him. Meanwhile the family really did grow from only a few to millions – a great nation. When it proved difficult for the Israelites in their many tribes and locations to identify with a King they couldn't see, God gave them a king as other nations had – David, and his sons – who pulled the tribes together into a force to be reckoned with on the international scene. It was the most glorious era in Jewish history.

The blessing – Here was the really amazing part of the Covenant. The curse of all mankind was death – the just punishment against sin. Here God was offering Abraham and his children – and through them to others in the rest of the world – the chance to be forgiven of their sins and be rescued from death. They would be brought back from death to life, and from separation from God to a close relationship with God. The Temple and its system of sacrifices made all of this possible.

As you can see, these promises summarize everything that a Jew holds dear. And now it's all gone. God has closed the doors to the Covenant so that no Jew can enjoy its promises now.

But in Jesus the entire Covenant is fulfilled – and Abraham himself knew that!

The promise of the Son – Abraham knew that his son Isaac wasn't the full promise that God had in mind, when the Lord promised to give him a son. We have proof of this from Jesus himself:

Your father Abraham rejoiced at the thought of seeing *my day*; he saw it and was glad. (John 8:56)

Isaac couldn't shoulder the responsibility of the Covenant estate – he was only a man, a sinner at that, and died himself after a few years. Jesus, however, lives forever to take care of all of Abraham's children. He has the treasures of Heaven at his disposal. He alone is sinless and has full access to God the Father. He is the only Heir who can get the rest of us into the presence of God.

The promise of the Land – Abraham also knew that the dusty piece of real estate called Canaan wasn't all that God had in mind when he promised him and his seed the land. Again, we don't have to guess what was in his mind; we have testimony from someone who was certain about how much Abraham knew about this matter:

By faith he made his home in the promised land like a stranger in a foreign country; he lived in tents, as did Isaac and Jacob, who were heirs with him of the same promise. For he was looking forward to the city with foundations, whose architect and builder is God. (Hebrews 11:9-10)

The real fulfillment of the Land was the place where God himself lives: in Heaven, far above all creation, the New Jerusalem, where God lives with his people and we will see him face to face and enjoy him and the joys of Heaven forever.

49

The promise of the Nation – We don't know how many people there are in Heaven now, but we do know that the number is growing. For example, we know that a man named Lazarus is one of them.

> At his gate was laid a beggar named Lazarus, covered with sores and longing to eat what fell from the rich man's table. Even the dogs came and licked his sores. The time came when the beggar died and the angels carried him to Abraham's side. (Luke 16:20-22)

But look again at the testimony of Jesus, who came from Heaven and is an eyewitness of what is going on there right now:

> I say to you that many will come from the east and the west, and will take their places at the feast with Abraham, Isaac and Jacob in the kingdom of Heaven. (Matthew 8:11)

The family of Abraham is getting larger, and they are gathering in Heaven for the great feast that God has planned for them. Perhaps Abraham was surprised to see so many Gentiles there, and so few of the Jews there! "But the subjects of the kingdom will be thrown outside, into the darkness, where there will be weeping and gnashing of teeth." (Matthew 8:12) At any rate he knows now exactly what God had in mind when he promised that he would become the father of a great nation. Both Jew and Gentile would become a New Man.

The promise of the Blessing – When Abraham came so close to sacrificing his son Isaac, he thought that death was certain. But he also knew that God wouldn't leave it that way. We already saw the testimony of Hebrews about this:

Abraham reasoned that God could raise the dead, and figuratively speaking, he did receive Isaac back from death. (Hebrews 11:19)

In other words, he learned something about God and his ways: the Lord intends to raise his promised children from the dead. Death will not be the end of us; we will live again, never to die again, to serve the Lord forever.

That's why the resurrection of Jesus Christ from the dead is so crucial for our faith. As the first of a new race of man, he was brought out of death into eternal life, and now lives with God the Father in Heaven. And when a person turns to Christ for the same salvation, he is assured of the same future.

So the Covenant to Abraham is perfectly fulfilled *spiritually*. We don't need the earthly promises anymore, because we have better and permanent promises to look forward to now.

• **The Name** – One of the most incredible events that ever happened in Jewish history concerns the Name Yahweh.

At the beginning of Israel's history as a nation, the Lord revealed his special Name to them. This God showed himself to be a Savior, a God who will have mercy on sinners who come to him and repent. We first learn what this particular Name means, and its importance to the Israelites, in Exodus:

51

The LORD, the LORD, the compassionate and gracious God, slow to anger, abounding in love and faithfulness, maintaining love to thousands, and forgiving wickedness, rebellion and sin. Yet he does not leave the guilty unpunished; he punishes the children and their children for the sin of the fathers to the third and fourth generation. (Exodus 34:6-7)

The Hebrew word being used here is יהוה. We can put it into English letters like this: YHWH. Our English translations usually render the word as "LORD" with all capital letters, to distinguish it from another word "Lord" from the Hebrew "Adon."

Around 400 BC the Jews were trying their best to follow the letter of the Law. They had just come back from exile in Babylon, having been sent there as punishment for their idolatry, and they were trying to behave themselves for a change. They took another look at the Third Commandment and decided that perhaps they weren't obeying it with all their hearts. So they *quit using* the Name of the Lord in daily conversation; they didn't want to risk offending him with a useless reference to him. Soon they quit using it even in religious services, claiming that the sinful lips of men ought not to profane the holy Name under *any* circumstances. They came up with all sorts of clever ways around having to pronounce the Name when reading the Scriptures. For example, they often substituted another word, like "Adonai," in its place so they wouldn't have to pronounce the holy Name that was written in the text.

You should know a little thing about Hebrew at this point. Written Hebrew was for a long time a language of consonants only; they never wrote the vowels in the text.

It's as if we would write the first sentence in this paragraph like this: **Y shld knw lttl thng bt Hbrw t ths pnt**. As you can see, most of the words are fairly easy to make out, but you probably would have trouble with some of them. The Jews didn't need written vowels, however, because everyone knew how to pronounce the words already.

The problem is that, since nobody was allowed to pronounce it, after a while they *all*, even the priests, forgot how to pronounce the special Name of God! YHWH is a word without consonants, so you can put in several different vowel combinations and they would work. But to this day nobody knows for sure how the Lord first pronounced it to Moses.

That's not the worst of it, however. Because of their over-zealous attitude about keeping the Law, they shut the door to the most powerful resource they had at their disposal. *They refused to call upon the Name of the LORD* — and therefore denied themselves all the good things that are in that Name, and the privileges that come from honoring God's Name. And this was in spite of the plain promise that God gave them about it.

> And everyone who calls on the Name of the LORD will be saved. (Joel 2:32)

When Solomon built the first temple, he knew that God Almighty wouldn't himself fit into a little stone building made by man! The Temple housed God in a special way.

> But will God really dwell on earth with men? The heavens, even the highest heavens, cannot contain you. How much less this temple I have built! Yet give attention to your servant's prayer

and his plea for mercy, O LORD my God. Hear the cry and the prayer that your servant is praying in your presence. May your eyes be open toward this temple day and night, this place of which you said *you would put your Name there.* May you hear the prayer your servant prays toward this place. (2 Chronicles 6:18-20)

The Jews were supposed to call on Yahweh for salvation; that was God's way of saving them and answering their prayers. But instead of laying hold of the very thing that would save them, they turned away from it (it's no matter whether they did it from stubbornness, superstition, or "reverence for the Name", because it amounts to the same thing) and died spiritually as a result. Long before Christ was born the Jews were wasting away because of their obstinacy; the prophecy about them came true:

No one calls on your Name or strives to lay hold of you; for you have hidden your face from us and made us waste away because of our sins. (Isaiah 64:7)

When Jesus dealt with the Jews he found a people slavishly following the letter of the Law, getting nowhere, straining out gnats and swallowing camels because they didn't understand the spiritual meaning of their Scriptures. All this because they refused to call on God's Name.

To this day the Jews are forbidden to pronounce the special Name of their God, even in synagogue services. For example, in 1985 the Jewish Publication Society put out a new translation of the Old Testament. In Leviticus 24:16, right after the story about Shelomith's son blaspheming God's Name, we read this in their translation:

> Anyone who blasphemes his God shall bear his guilt; if he also pronounces the name LORD [*which is **Yahweh**, the name that Jews think they're not allowed to say*], he shall be put to death. The whole community shall stone him; stranger or citizen, if he has thus pronounced the Name, he shall be put to death.

This is an example of deliberately mistranslating a passage in order to support a tradition. The Hebrew word behind "pronounce" in this Jewish translation is נקב – which actually means "curse, blaspheme," a meaning given by the leading Hebrew dictionaries available. In fact, the dictionary by Brown, Driver & Briggs [2] specifically states that it means "curse" here in this Leviticus passage – not "pronounce!" It's a real shame that the Jews are so desperate to keep their tradition that they purposely change the meaning of the Bible. One is reminded of Jesus' condemnation of their fathers for the same sin:

> And he said to them: "You have a fine way of setting aside the commands of God in order to observe your own traditions!" (Mark 7:9)

The Hebrew name Joshua (יְהוֹשֻׁעַ) is actually the same name that Jesus had.

---

[2] *Hebrew and English Lexicon of the Old Testament*, Brown, Driver & Briggs: Oxford.

Greek	Hebrew
Jesus (Ἰησοῦς)	**Joshua** (יְהוֹשֻׁעַ)

"Jesus" is the Greek form of *Yehoshua*, or Joshua. So if Jesus would have lived in Old Testament times, he would have been called Joshua; and if Joshua had lived in New Testament times he would have been called Jesus.

The name **Yehoshua** is a combination of two words –

"Yah" (short for **Yahweh**, or יהוה), and ...

"yasha" (ישע) which means "to save"

So both "Jesus" and "Joshua" mean "Yahweh saves."

In Jesus the Name has been revived. There is the connection between Jesus of the New Testament and the LORD of the Old Testament — that same Name reveals the same God at work. It's no wonder then that Jesus was such a perfect example of the God who is "compassionate and gracious, slow to anger, abounding in love and faithfulness!"

Remember what Peter said about the Name of Christ? "Salvation is found in no one else, for there is no other Name under Heaven given to men by which we must be saved." (Acts 4:12) When he said that to Jews, they should have flinched — they knew the utter holiness of the Name, and they were jealous for its glory. Here was Peter claiming the same glory for Jesus' Name! He was calling up visions of the God of the Old Testament, the one to whom the Israelites called for help in their time of need. He was claiming that Jesus would save us just as the LORD did in the Old Testament, because we are dealing with the same God. The only difference now is that we can see our God, and touch him, and hear him clearly as he speaks to us. His power and ability to save his people remain the same, however.

- **The Book** – The Bible is pretty much the only thing that God left the Jews in 70 AD; everything else was destroyed or taken away from them. But as if to emphasize the spiritually destitute condition of the Jews, the Lord closed their minds to the true meaning of their Bible so that they cannot understand it now. So the Jews have set aside the Bible and have replaced it with inferior writings.

Besides the Old Testament (which to the Jews is the "Bible" – it's the Old Testament only to us Christians) the Jews hold the **Mishnah** and the **Talmud** to be sacred literature. It's a real education to read through the Talmud. The Talmud is a collection of "tractates" or books that deal with the laws of Judaism. Basically it's an extended commentary on the Law of Moses – as well as their own additions to the Law, discussions, arguments, legal decisions, and so on. One modern edition of the Talmud consists of 20 large volumes.

To the Jews, the Talmud is indispensable to their faith, because they feel that the Law of Moses in itself is too condensed, too generic for use in daily life. The Talmud explores how to live the Law in today's society – it makes applications of the Law to everyday life.

The essence of Judaism entails carefully weighing the applicability of traditional principles in encountering daily dilemmas.[3]

Because this makes their religion practical and "do-able," the Talmud – and scholars who know the Talmud – are absolutely central to the Jewish faith. They control Judaism.

Here is an example from the Talmud of the rabbinical arguments – the way they argued and what they liked to argue about. As you can see, it is difficult reading.

It has been taught: The blasphemer is not punished unless he "blesses" the Name, by the Name. Whence do we know this? – Samuel said: The Writ sayeth, *And he that blasphemeth the name of the Lord ... when he blasphemeth the name of the Lord, shall be put to death*. How do you know that the word used in the Hebrew means a "blessing"? – From the verse, *How shall I curse whom God hath not cursed*; whilst the formal prohibition is contained in the verse, *thou shalt not revile God*. But perhaps it means "to pierce," as it is written, *So Jehoiada the priest took a chest, and bored a hole in the lid of it*, the formal injunction against this being the verses, *Ye shall destroy the names of the idols out of that place. Ye shall not do so unto the Lord your God?* – The Name must be "blessed" by the Name, which is absent here. But perhaps the text refers to the putting of two slips of parchment, each bearing the Divine Name, together, and piercing them both? – In that case one

[3] *The Talmud: Selected Writings* (trans. Ben Zion Bokser; Paulist Press: New York; 1989); p. 11.

Name is pierced after the other. But perhaps it prohibits the engraving of the Divine Name on the point of a knife and piercing therewith the Divine Name written on a slip of parchment? – In that case the point of the knife pierces, not the Divine Name. But perhaps it refers to the pronunciation of the ineffable Name, as it is written, *And Moses and Aaron took these men which are expressed by their names*; the formal prohibition being contained in the verse, *Thou shalt fear the Lord thy God?* – Firstly, the Name must be "blessed" by the Name, which is absent here; and secondly, it is a prohibition in the form of a positive command, which is not deemed to be a prohibition at all. An alternative answer is this: The Write saith, *And the Israelitish woman's son blasphemed and cursed*, proving that blasphemy denotes cursing. But perhaps it teaches that both offences must be perpetrated? You cannot think so, because it is written, *Bring forth him that hath cursed*, and not "him that has blasphemed and cursed," proving that no offence only is alluded to.[4]

But when you flip through the pages of the Talmud, you will look in vain for a detailed discussion of any kind of *spiritual* world. The focus of Jewish holy books is on *this physical world* – it doesn't appear to be concerned about Heaven, or living in the light that shines down from Heaven through the Bible. The Talmud only sees the physical; it appears to be blind to spiritual realities. For example, here is how the Talmud is broken down:

---

[4] *Hebrew-English Edition of the Babylonian Talmud:* Tractate Sanhedrin; Soncino Press: London; 1994; p. 56a.

Section 1: *Zera'im* ("Seeds"): This deals mostly with blessings and prayers, the tithes that must be set aside for the priests and poor, and land-related regulations (sabbatical years, mixed sowing, etc.).

Section 2: *Mo'ed* ("Festivals"): This deals with the weekly Sabbath observance and the cycle of annual festivals.

Section 3: *Nashim* ("Women"): This section concerns marriage, divorce, etc., including the laws of oaths.

Section 4: *Neziqin* ("Torts"): This covers the civil and criminal laws, including the structure of the judiciary, as well as the history of Rabbinic authority.

Section 5: *Qodashim* ("Sacred Things"): This describes the Temple and sacrificial worship.

Section 6: *Tohorot* ("Purity"): This section deals with the rules of purity.

The problem of the Talmud started after the return from Exile in Babylon. The Jews claim that there arose in Israel an "oral Law" alongside the Law that they received from God through Moses. It consisted of practical applications of the Mosaic Law: they realized that the old Mosaic Law was peculiar to the former days before the Exile, and living in changing cultures demanded new ways of applying the Law to suit the circumstances. So the leaders of the community devised more laws, more regulations, and even memorized the very arguments that were used to hash out these new laws. Thus arose the

Mishnah – a commentary and expansion on the Law of Moses. Eventually they were overwhelmed by the bulk of material and they wrote it down before anyone forgot it.

Then the process started all over again – the Jews weren't satisfied that the Mishnah covered all possible ways that the Law could be applied to life. They had more arguments, more scholars who dug deeper into the Law, more disputed points of application – and ever more laws. As this body of material grew – a kind of commentary and expansion of the Mishnah itself – it became known as the Talmud.

The Mishnah is a large volume of legal proceedings and decisions. The Talmud, in modern editions, is a set of many volumes of arguments, legal proceedings and decisions. The Jews value these two sets highly, often more than the original Biblical Law itself. In fact, the Talmud describes the Jewish religion as we know it today; no Jew would be comfortable with identifying with just the Mosaic Law. The Talmud is modern Judaism; they no longer look like the Israelites of the Old Testament. They see themselves in the Talmud, developing into a unique culture over the centuries, codifying their beliefs and traditions. Without the Talmud, Judaism as it has come to be known would be impossible. Scholars of the Talmud are highly regarded in the Jewish community.

No book in the history of Judaism, not even the Bible, has had the formative influence of the Talmud. Everything in the history of Judaism that predates the Talmud seems incomplete and unfinished, while everything that comes after the Talmud seems a mere supplement to it. [5]

---

[5] *The Talmud: Selected Writings*; p. 3.

In case after case, the careful study of talmudic legal discussion reveals that there is no real law at all, and thus no useful statement of God's will, until the *rabbinic authorities* have decided what the law is to be … The collective of the Sages, and no one else, now determine the meaning of Torah. The Torah is no longer "in heaven"; *even its heavenly Giver can no longer interfere* in the process of interpreting it, applying it, and expanding its scope. [6]

Notice several points about this claim: **first**, that the Jews alone understand the Law. **Second**, that nobody can understand the Law of Moses (Genesis through Deuteronomy) without the Talmud. **Third**, that they have a divine calling to interpret the Law through the Talmud. **Fourth**, that even God submits to their interpretation of the Law in the Talmud. Pretty arrogant claims, aren't they? The trouble is that none of their claims are true.

The Jews can't follow the Law of Moses; that we have already seen. They give lip service to the Law but they don't order their lives by it. They have replaced their Scriptures with the Talmud, which is useless for their spiritual state – there's no forgiveness there, no cleansing of the soul, only outward ceremonies and legal wrangling over nonessentials.

Now that Jesus has come, however, we can understand the real meaning of the Jewish Bible – it's all a description of him and his ministry. He first told the Jews that they didn't understand their own Bible.

---

[6] Ibid., p. 5. Italics ours.

You diligently study the Scriptures because you think that by them you possess eternal life. These are the Scriptures that testify about me, yet you refuse to come to me to have life. (John 5:39-40)

You have a fine way of setting aside the commands of God in order to observe your own traditions! (Mark 7:9)

Paul says that there's a veil that covers the Jewish mind when they hear the Scriptures read. They can't see the spiritual point there; only Christians can truly understand the true meaning of the Old Testament.

But their minds were made dull, for to this day the same veil remains when the old covenant is read. It has not been removed, because only in Christ is it taken away. Even to this day when Moses is read, a veil covers their hearts. But whenever anyone turns to the Lord, the veil is taken away. (2 Corinthians 3:14-16)

It's the hand of God. He closed their minds so that the only things they see in the Bible are words – springboards for legal wranglings.

What Israel sought so earnestly it did not obtain, but the elect did. The others were hardened, as it is written: "God gave them a spirit of stupor, eyes so that they could not see and ears so that they could not hear, to this very day." (Romans 11:7-8)

Paul, however, a trained Pharisee who was taught by the Spirit of God, learned the true meaning of the Old Testament.

… The holy Scriptures, which are able to make you wise for salvation through faith in Christ Jesus. (2 Timothy 3:15)

The experience of God's people in the Old Testament was a shadow, a pattern, a physical lesson in which someone with "eyes to see" could learn about God's spiritual world and how it really works. That's why Jesus expected the Jews to be ready for him when he came to lift his people from the physical to the spiritual. They should have understood him perfectly, having gone through the lessons. Instead, being blind to the real point of their Bible, they turned away from Jesus the Savior and jumped even deeper into their tangled mass of legalisms. They should not have been so blind as to mistake the shadow for the reality, however!

Now there was a man of the Pharisees named Nicodemus, a member of the Jewish ruling council. He came to Jesus at night and said, "Rabbi, we know you are a teacher who has come from God. For no one could perform the miraculous signs you are doing if God were not with him."

In reply Jesus declared, "I tell you the truth, no one can see the kingdom of God unless he is born again."

"How can a man be born when he is old?" Nicodemus asked. "Surely he cannot enter a second time into his mother's womb to be born!"

Jesus answered, "I tell you the truth, no one can enter the kingdom of God unless he is born of water and the Spirit. Flesh gives birth to flesh, but the Spirit gives birth to spirit. You should not be surprised at my saying, 'You must be born again.' The wind blows wherever it pleases. You hear its sound, but you cannot tell where it comes from or where it is going. So it is with everyone born of the Spirit."

"How can this be?" Nicodemus asked.

"You are Israel's teacher," said Jesus, "and do you not understand these things?" (John 3:1-10)

The lesson to learn

When God takes away something precious from us, it's for a reason. Usually it's because we need to be disciplined, or taught the value of something we were taking for granted, or steered out of trouble into a safer direction.

The Jews have never satisfactorily explained why they lost everything 2000 years ago. Their standard answer has been that they were victims of their enemies – that their entire history has been plagued by enemies who are out to destroy them. They long for the day when God will vindicate them and return them to their home and Biblical roots. In the meantime, they claim, they have become "people of the Book" – because the Bible is all that they have left.

The problem with this explanation is twofold: first, whatever they think of their enemies, it still doesn't explain how they think that they can be good Jews – in other words, how they can please God with their religion – when they can't carry out the major requirements of their religion. Without the Temple, and the Covenant promises, and genealogical records, all their worship (according to the Book) is unacceptable to God. They can't just take a pragmatic attitude toward it all and say "Oh, well, we'll just have to make do with what we have" when their own Law continues to condemn them for not following the Law to the letter!

Second, they haven't even got the Book anymore. The Talmud has effectively replaced their Bible and made a new religion out of Judaism. It had to – all the old foundations were taken away, so the Jews created man-made traditions to fill the void. For example, instead of relying on the High Priest's ministry on the Day of Atonement in the Holy of Holies, the Jews of today simply plead with God to weigh their good deeds against their bad ones and hope in his mercy to be written in his Book of Life. The Talmud recommends this approach because the method of atonement for sin, recorded in the Torah, is useless to them now.

A thoughtful Jew should be asking at this point: why did God take these things away from us? Why did he destroy the nation, scatter them around the world, destroy the Temple and its sacrifices, and bring everything Jewish to an end? What is he trying to say?

God is trying to say that none of this is needed anymore!

Think it through. If the Law absolutely required a Temple, because it's God's house where he will live with his people and they can approach him there; if it absolutely required blood sacrifice for sin; if it promised the Covenant blessings of Abraham only to those who could prove descendancy to father Abraham – then would God suddenly change his mind and not require these things? Is God so capricious that one day he puts people to death for not obeying the Law to the letter, and the next day he dissolves the Law and tells people to do whatever they want as a replacement? Not so! The only obvious conclusion to draw from the destructive events of the first century is that they are no longer needed – there is a better, permanent, and spiritual system that takes the place of the old system, yet keeps the intent of the original.

For instance, the earthly Temple (or Tabernacle as Moses originally made it) was patterned after the one in Heaven.

> They serve at a sanctuary that is a copy and shadow of what is in Heaven. This is why Moses was warned when he was about to build the tabernacle: "See to it that you make everything according to the pattern shown you on the mountain." (Hebrews 8:5)

> Then God's temple in Heaven was opened, and within his temple was seen the ark of his covenant. (Revelation 11:19)

Why, then, would we need a Temple in Jerusalem when God has his home in Heaven already? The one thing that man has desperately needed was access to this Temple; all he wants to do is find God. For a time (1500 years) God condescended to live in a copy of his Temple in Canaan, so that the Israelites could learn what it's like to live with God, and they could find him there. Now, however, since Jesus gives us his Spirit, we have the ability to enter the Throne Room *in Heaven* and find God *there*.

> But you have come to Mount Zion, to the Heavenly Jerusalem, the city of the living God. You have come to thousands upon thousands of angels in joyful assembly, to the church of the firstborn, whose names are written in heaven. You have come to God, the judge of all men, to the spirits of righteous men made perfect, to Jesus the mediator of a new covenant, and to the sprinkled blood that speaks a better word than the blood of Abel. (Hebrews 12:22-24)

For a time, the land of Canaan was home for the Jews. It was far better than the slavery of Egypt; it was a land "flowing with milk and honey," nestled safely in the hills of Palestine.

But why would people choose Palestine now, with its desert conditions and water problems and surrounded by enemies, when we can have a Promised Land in God's world free of the problems of sin and death and overflowing with unimaginable wealth and pleasures?

And he carried me away in the Spirit to a mountain great and high, and showed me the Holy City, Jerusalem, coming down out of Heaven from God. It shone with the glory of God, and its brilliance was like that of a very precious jewel, like a jasper, clear as crystal. (Revelation 21:10-11)

I did not see a temple in the city, because the Lord God Almighty and the Lamb are its temple. The city does not need the sun or the moon to shine on it, for the glory of God gives it light, and the Lamb is its lamp. The nations will walk by its light, and the kings of the earth will bring their splendor into it. On no day will its gates ever be shut, for there will be no night there. The glory and honor of the nations will be brought into it. Nothing impure will ever enter it, nor will anyone who does what is shameful or deceitful, but only those whose names are written in the Lamb's book of life.

Then the angel showed me the river of the water of life, as clear as crystal, flowing from the throne of God and of the Lamb down the middle of the great street of the city. On each side of the river stood the tree of life, bearing twelve crops of fruit, yielding its fruit every month. And the leaves of the tree are for the healing of the nations. No longer will there be any curse. The throne of

God and of the Lamb will be in the city, and his servants will serve him. They will see his face, and his Name will be on their foreheads. There will be no more night. They will not need the light of a lamp or the light of the sun, for the Lord God will give them light. And they will reign for ever and ever. (Revelation 21:22 – 22:5)

We don't even have to worry about how to get there. Jesus has a way planned to take us to Heaven when we leave this world, and God the Father is waiting for us.

> In my Father's house are many rooms; if it were not so, I would have told you. I am going there to prepare a place for you. And if I go and prepare a place for you, I will come back and take you to be with me that you also may be where I am. You know the way to the place where I am going. (John 14:2-4)

The sacrifice for sin in the Old Testament – the blood of animals – never did take sin away from their hearts, and the Israelites knew that. They should have known that there must be a more permanent solution to the stubborn stain of sin; God wouldn't leave its removal to us alone.

> The blood of goats and bulls and the ashes of a heifer sprinkled on those who are ceremonially unclean sanctify them so that they are outwardly clean. How much more, then, will the blood of Christ, who through the eternal Spirit offered himself unblemished to God, cleanse our consciences from acts that lead to death, so that we may serve the living God! (Hebrews 9:13-14)

> The Law is only a shadow of the good things that are coming – not the realities themselves. For this reason it can never, by the same sacrifices repeated endlessly year after year, make perfect those who draw near to worship.

If it could, would they not have stopped being offered? For the worshipers would have been cleansed once for all, and would no longer have felt guilty for their sins. But those sacrifices are an annual reminder of sins, because it is impossible for the blood of bulls and goats to take away sins. Therefore, when Christ came into the world, he said: "Sacrifice and offering you did not desire, but a body you prepared for me; with burnt offerings and sin offerings you were not pleased. Then I said, 'Here I am – it is written about me in the scroll – I have come to do your will, O God.'" First he said, "Sacrifices and offerings, burnt offerings and sin offerings you did not desire, nor were you pleased with them" (although the Law required them to be made). Then he said, "Here I am, I have come to do your will." He sets aside the first to establish the second. And by that will, we have been made holy through the sacrifice of the body of Jesus Christ once for all. (Hebrews 10:1-10)

Trust in Jesus, and his sacrifice will erase all records of your sin, and his righteousness will fill your heart to make you perfect as he is.

And you needn't worry about your genealogy either, whether you can prove your descent from Abraham in order to inherit the promises given him by God. Nobody now can prove their family tree back to Abraham or any of the tribes of Israel – the families have intermarried, names have been long lost, there is absolutely no record anymore. But if you are one with Christ through faith in him, then you are "plugged into" the family (by virtue of the fact that *he* is the Son and heir of Abraham) and all the promises are now yours as well. The whole thing is so easy now, and it solves all the problems.

So the Law was put in charge to lead us to Christ that we might be justified by faith. Now that faith has come, we are no longer under the supervision of the Law. You are all sons of God through faith in Christ Jesus, for all of you who were baptized into Christ have clothed yourselves with Christ. There is neither Jew nor Greek, slave nor free, male nor female, for you are all one in Christ Jesus. *If you belong to Christ, then you are Abraham's seed, and heirs according to the promise.* (Galatians 3:24-29)

Christians have known about these spiritual truths for 2000 years. They've been taking advantage of the promises by believing in Jesus. Jesus brings them into the spiritual world of God where all these things and more are real, and they can get a "foretaste" of things to come in Heaven.

One of the most important aspects of the Bible is how the physical and spiritual levels interact with each other in the timeline of God's works.

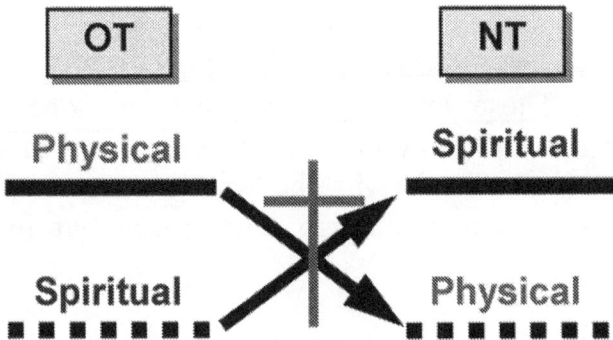

Physical versus Spiritual

In the Old Testament, the physical level predominates. We see animal sacrifices in a physical Temple. We see the children of Israel settling down in Canaan. We watch David pulling the tribes together and defeating the Moabites and Philistines. Just about everything we read about is something that we can see, feel, or hear with our physical senses.

In the New Testament, the spiritual level predominates. The situation flip-flops, so to speak. Now instead of a physical Temple, we learn of the Temple in Heaven that we must come to. Now instead of a physical land of Canaan to inherit, we inherit Heaven. David sitting on throne in Jerusalem turns into the Son of David sitting on his throne beside the Father. The Philistines aren't a problem to us anymore, but our sins and the "spiritual forces of darkness" certainly are.

Of course the situation in the Old Testament was also spiritual, but they were required to learn and work things out through the physical means that God gave them. Only by faith would they realize that a more permanent solution would eventually come to light. Now, however, the veil has been taken away, the time has come; the eternal solution has been revealed to us.

We don't need the physical anymore. It has served its purpose; the lessons are now recorded in the Old Testament for all to learn. Those lessons are a stepping stone, a primer to something better. Why long for the shadow when you can have the real thing? That's why the Apostles urged us to leave the physical behind and, through faith, reach out for the eternal realities.

The Jews have been longing to return to their old system. But what they need to realize is that God did away with the old system, replaced it with a new one, and is now offering it to *all who will come* – to both Jew and Gentile. Everyone has access to it now on the same basis, the same opportunity, by coming to Jesus Christ the door to Heaven. He is the key that gives access to the spiritual realities that the Old Testament system pointed to.

But now in Christ Jesus you who once were far away have been brought near through the blood of Christ. For he himself is our peace, who has made the two one and has destroyed the barrier, the dividing wall of hostility, by abolishing in his flesh the Law with its commandments and regulations. His purpose was to create in himself one new man out of the two, thus making peace, and in this one body to reconcile both of them to God through the cross, by which he put to death their hostility. He came and preached peace to you who were far away and peace to those who were near. For through him we both have access to the Father by one Spirit. Consequently, you are no longer foreigners and aliens, but fellow citizens with God's people and members of God's household, built on the foundation of the Apostles and prophets, with Christ Jesus himself as the chief cornerstone. In him the whole building is joined together and rises to become a holy temple in the Lord. And in him you too are being built together to become a dwelling in which God lives by his Spirit. (Ephesians 2:13-22)

Just as Paul said, the natural, physical system of the Jews was only for a time, to teach God's people the principles of the Kingdom. It cannot be the eternal, spiritual system that all of God's people need now. It has been resurrected from the dead.

Flesh and blood cannot inherit the kingdom of God, nor does the perishable inherit the imperishable. (1 Corinthians 15:50)

The body that is sown is perishable, it is raised imperishable; it is sown in dishonor, it is raised in glory; it is sown in weakness, it is raised in power; it is sown a natural body, it is raised a spiritual body. If there is a natural body, there is also a spiritual body. (1 Corinthians 15:42-44)

Why a Jew cannot be a good Jew

Christians and Tithing

Christians and Tithing

Tithing is a touchy subject. People have argued for and against tithing for centuries, and still it seems that Christians aren't at all agreed on what God requires of us. Since it affects our pocketbooks we'd like to know; we certainly don't want to put hard earned money into an organization that man is running in his own way, for his own ends, that doesn't help to advance the Kingdom of God. There are, sadly, too many instances of that sort of thing going on – and they were faithfully financed by people who were told that it was their duty to support the work with "their tithes and offerings." On the positive side, there are many churches that are really trying to advance God's Kingdom; but again they appeal to "tithing" to finance the church's needs and they use certain Scriptures to prove that each Christian is obligated to tithe to the Lord's work.

There are many who would doubt the wisdom of questioning one of the time-honored traditions of the Church. But for that very reason we need to look at tithing again, in light of the Scriptures, to test its worth. If it's our duty then we will lose nothing by studying it again. But if we've been misinformed then it's better that we find that out now instead of continuing to follow a tradition that the Bible may actually teach against.

Another reason we are justified in looking at it is because church leaders often bind people's consciences with this requirement. If they don't actually say it from the pulpit that Christians are obligated to tithe – and they will provide certain Scriptures as proof – then they will "persuade" their people to consider what the Bible "teaches us to do" – with the idea that the Lord is not only pleased with a "cheerful giver" but especially with a tithing Christian.

I have no argument with the "cheerful giver" concept; it's the idea of "tithing," as defined in the Scriptures, that I differ from their position. In this study we will look at what the Bible says about tithing, hopefully coming to an understanding of what God really wants us to know about it.

The word "tithe"

The word "tithe" is based on the Hebrew word 'sr, a root that means "to gather together, to unite." From that word grew a group of nouns that have to do with the number 10 – *'eser*, which means "ten," and *'asar*, which is a verb meaning "to take the tenth part of." (*A Hebrew and English Lexicon of the Old Testament*, Brown, Driver & Briggs; pp. 796-797)

I'm afraid that we modern Americans don't appreciate the fullness of the imagery of tithing as the Hebrews understood it. When we write a check, it's just a matter of giving away some of our money, which is sitting in the bank, to another person. But to the Israelites it wasn't the same kind of process. "Payday" for them was an important agricultural event; their riches were literally crops and animals, not dollars in the bank. To use their riches in any way meant that they had to go out and "gather together" the grain or sheep. When they harvested their fields, which was a yearly event and brought neighbors and relatives together in a big gala social affair, they cut the grain and piled it into heaps for storage for the winter.

Tithing wasn't just a matter of juggling numbers in a bank account. When harvest began, they collected a tenth of the field's grain first and made a separate pile, then the rest was gathered after that. The Levites came to each family's field and picked up their tithe, and took it to the Temple in Jerusalem. The tithe was a very real thing, then, as they saw it sitting there apart from the rest of the harvest – it was "holy to the Lord." So you can see why the

Hebrew word came from the idea of "gathering together." You can also see why tithing was an important event to them, an event which happened at harvest time, shearing time and butchering time – not at the weekly intervals that we use to give our money to the church. Their practice reflected their culture.

What is the Law?

The Law concerning tithing can be found in these passages:

A tithe of everything from the land, whether grain from the soil or fruit from the trees, belongs to the LORD; it is holy to the LORD. If a man redeems any of his tithe, he must add a fifth of the value to it. The entire tithe of the herd and flock—every tenth animal that passes under the shepherd's rod—will be holy to the LORD. He must not pick out the good from the bad or make any substitution. If he does make a substitution, both the animal and its substitute become holy and cannot be redeemed. (Leviticus 27:30-33)

The LORD said to Moses, "Speak to the Levites and say to them: 'When you receive from the Israelites the tithe I give you as your inheritance, you must present a tenth of that tithe as the LORD's offering. Your offering will be reckoned to you as grain from the threshing floor or juice from the winepress. In this way you also will present an offering to the LORD from all the tithes you receive from the Israelites. From these tithes you must give the LORD's portion to Aaron the priest. You must present as the LORD's portion the best and holiest part of everything given to you.' " (Numbers 18:25-29)

You must not eat in your own towns the tithe of your grain and new wine and oil, or the firstborn of your herds and flocks, or whatever you have vowed to give, or your freewill offerings or special gifts. Instead, you are to eat them in the presence of the LORD your God at the place the LORD your God will choose — you, your sons and daughters, your menservants and maidservants, and the Levites from your towns — and you are to rejoice before the LORD your God in everything you put your hand to. Be careful not to neglect the Levites as long as you live in your land. (Deuteronomy 12:17-19)

Be sure to set aside a tenth of all that your fields produce each year. Eat the tithe of your grain, new wine and oil, and the firstborn of your herds and flocks in the presence of the LORD your God at the place he will choose as a dwelling for his Name, so that you may learn to revere the LORD your God always. But if that place is too distant and you have been blessed by the LORD your God and cannot carry your tithe (because the place where the LORD will choose to put his Name is so far away), then exchange your tithe for silver, and take the silver with you and go to the place the LORD your God will choose. Use the silver to buy whatever you like: cattle, sheep, wine or other fermented drink, or anything you wish. Then you and your household shall eat there in the presence of the LORD your God and rejoice. And do not neglect the Levites living in your towns, for they have no allotment or inheritance of their own. At the end of every three years, bring all the tithes of that year's produce and store it in your towns, so that the Levites (who have no allotment or inheritance of their own) and the aliens, the fatherless and the widows who live in your towns may come and eat and be satisfied, and so that the LORD your God may bless you in all the work of your hands. (Deuteronomy 14:22-29)

The passages were given in full because of the details involved. Notice several things about the Law of tithing:

- *First*, because it was the Law of God given to the Israelites at Mt. Sinai, there were no exceptions. They had to obey the Law to the letter. "These are the commands the LORD gave Moses on Mount Sinai for the Israelites" (Leviticus 27:34) – a verse which comes immediately after the Law of tithing. Tithing is to be done exactly as this Law describes, in this way, for these purposes only. And as we know from other examples of the Law, there is no room for changing the Law's requirements to suit our own purposes. (See Leviticus 10:1-7 for an example of someone who tried!)

- *Second*, the tithes generally were taken to the Temple storehouses. The only exception was that on every third year they were collected locally and stored for the use of the Levites and other special groups. The point is that, for the most part, all of Israel took their tithe to the Temple. We will see the significance of this later.

- *Third*, the Law specifically commands the Israelites to *eat their tithe*. Each family was to eat their own tithe at the Temple – during the several festival times of the Jewish year. You may have wondered what those hundreds of thousands, perhaps millions of people ate when they all converged on Jerusalem during Passover! This Law explains the mystery. Everyone had something to eat during the festivals because they sent enough ahead of time to Jerusalem – a tenth was calculated to be enough for the circumstances – for themselves, the poor, the Levites, everyone. The purpose of the tithe is made clearer by an additional clause in the Law: if they grew so much grain and animals that it was too bulky to haul to Jerusalem, they could sell it in their home towns – cash is more easily carried over the long distance to Jerusalem than bulky cargo – and then buy whatever they needed for the feast when they reached the city. "Buy whatever you like" refers to getting food, drink, supplies and so on for their holiday stay in Jerusalem.

- *Fourth*, every third year the Israelites were supposed to gather their tithe locally in their own towns and distribute it among the Levites, the aliens, the fatherless and the widows. The point is clear: these are people who couldn't provide for themselves, and the tithe was to support them. The Lord prohibited the Levites from having any ancestral land like the other tribes had, so they had no way of growing crops or raising herds. The aliens had a tough time too, living in a strange land as they were. The fatherless and widows felt the loss of the men-folk keenly in matters of simple survival.

We can't get into a full blown discussion here on the nature of their religious feasts, nor the way that their society worked in taking care of those in need. But keeping in mind that those were very important issues to the Israelites (because they were important to God!), we can state – based on this Law from Sinai – that the tithe served a critical function in keeping both of these social systems running smoothly. Without the tithe, the festivals would never have worked (the Jews in Jerusalem, with their limited resources, just couldn't handle the crowds coming in from all over the nation), and the poor and the disadvantaged would have gone hungry. The Law, in other words, made sure that everything would work according to God's plan, which is the whole purpose of the Law.

The reason that the Law of tithing was sacrificial – the reason that the people had to be told to do it, otherwise they would have ignored it – is because it was tempting to keep that food and profit in one's own barn, instead of hauling it off to Jerusalem to be consumed. True to human nature, the Israelites would have rather kept their profits and presumed on the good will of others during the feasts in Jerusalem. Not so, the Lord commands! Everyone will contribute, nobody will hold back, everyone will share the load during the worship times. Wherever there is a tendency for greed, there is a Law to guard against it so that God's will might be done.

Other taxes

The tithe wasn't the only tax that the Law imposed on the Israelites. In 2 Chronicles we find this passage:

Why haven't you required the Levites to bring in from Judah and Jerusalem the tax imposed by Moses the servant of the LORD and by the assembly of Israel for the Tent of the Testimony? (2 Chronicles 24:6)

The parallel passage that we find in Kings spells out what those taxes were:

Collect all the money that is brought as sacred offerings to the temple of the LORD — the money collected in the census, the money received from personal vows and the money brought voluntarily to the temple. (2 Kings 12:4)

These are references to specific laws in the Mosaic Covenant. They were mandatory for all Jews, and they made possible all the necessary sacrifices and functions in the Temple:

Then the LORD said to Moses, "When you take a census of the Israelites to count them, each one must pay the LORD a ransom for his life at the time he is counted. Then no plague will come on them when you number them. Each one who crosses over to those already counted is to give a half shekel, according to the sanctuary shekel, which weighs twenty gerahs. This half shekel is an offering to the LORD. All who cross over, those twenty years old or more, are to give an offering to the LORD. The rich are not to give more than a half shekel and the poor are not to give less when you make the offering to the LORD to atone for your lives. Receive the atonement money from the Israelites and use it for the service of the Tent of Meeting. It will be a memorial for the Israelites before the LORD, making atonement for your lives." (Exodus 30:11-16)

The first offspring of every womb, both man and animal, that is offered to the LORD is yours. But you must redeem every firstborn son and every firstborn male of unclean animals. When they are a month old, you must redeem them at the redemption price set at five shekels of silver, according to the sanctuary shekel, which weighs twenty gerahs. (Numbers 18:15-16)

These passages also have interesting details. First, notice that they were mandatory – all Jews were obligated to pay these taxes. Second, they were set figures; there was no guessing about how much the Lord wanted them to pay. Third, the money was used for Temple expenses – grounds, furniture, repairs, supplies, etc.

Additional passages

In order to finish laying the Scriptural groundwork for the subject of tithing, let's look at a few more passages. First, the most famous passage in the Old Testament on the subject of tithing is in Malachi:

Will a man rob God? Yet you rob me. But you ask, 'How do we rob you?' In tithes and offerings. You are under a curse — the whole nation of you — because you are robbing me. Bring the whole tithe into the storehouse, that there may be food in my house. Test me in this, says the LORD Almighty, and see if I will not throw open the floodgates of Heaven and pour out so much blessing that you will not have room enough for it. (Malachi 3:8-10)

The story of Melchizedek, who was a priest and king that Abraham honored, also refers to tithing:

Then Melchizedek king of Salem brought out bread and wine. He was priest of God Most High, and he blessed Abram, saying, "Blessed be Abram by God Most High, Creator of Heaven and earth. And blessed be God Most High, who delivered your enemies into your hand." Then Abram gave him a tenth of everything. (Genesis 14:18-20)

Additional passages, that reflect more of what was already given in the passages above, are these: Genesis 28:22; 2 Chronicles 31:5-6; Nehemiah 10:37-38.

We will need one more passage for our discussion later on:

I give to the Levites all the tithes in Israel as their inheritance in return for the work they do while serving at the Tent of Meeting. From now on the Israelites must not go near the Tent of Meeting, or they will bear the consequences of their sin and will die. It is the Levites who are to do the work at the Tent of Meeting and bear the responsibility for offenses against it. This is a lasting ordinance for the generations to come. They will receive no inheritance among the Israelites. Instead, I give to the Levites as their inheritance the tithes that the Israelites present as an offering to the Lord. That is why I said concerning them: 'They will have no inheritance among the Israelites.' (Numbers 18:21-24)

Does this apply to Christians?

Now, the question that we have to answer is this: are these passages mandatory for the Christian? Are these laws something that church leaders can and, in fact, ought to, impose on the members of a church? Are we required to pay the tithe that the Old Testament speaks about?

The last question pretty much suggests its own answer. *As the tithe is described in the Old Testament, we Christians are not obligated to keep it.* But then I don't know anybody who does! The Old Testament Law specifically stated what people were to do with the tithe – *they were to eat it themselves.* The tithe was gathered throughout Israel, brought *to the Temple* in Jerusalem, and eaten there during the religious feasts as outlined in the Law. People could sell their tithe and carry the money to Jerusalem, but then they had to buy food and drink and necessities for the ceremonies so that they could obey the Law and eat their tithe.

Money wasn't the issue. It's true that their economic system was based on barter and ours is based on currency. But notice that they were allowed to sell their goods for currency if they wished – they could get money if they wanted to – but only for the purpose of buying food again when they arrived in Jerusalem. They weren't supposed to bring money to the Temple as a tithe, only food.

Part of the tithe went to the Levites, the aliens, the orphans and widows. This was a regular allotment and was *mandatory*. By Law, these people could expect something to live on because their neighbors were regularly taxed for it.

There just isn't any way we can stretch these Laws to fit our circumstances today. The word "tithe" nowadays is used strictly for money; it's brought to individual churches, not to the Temple of God; it's used for the building maintenance, salaries, supplies, mission programs, etc. – not for the use of the people themselves who gave the tithe, and certainly not to eat!

Someone might answer, "You're being picky. A church does need this money, and many of its needs resemble the circumstances of the Temple." Yes, many of its needs are the same. But my point is that the purpose of the *tithe* was so that the Israelites could eat at the religious festivals held at the Temple in Jerusalem. Though a case could be made (though a very shaky one, at best!) for saving a tenth of one's income, and bringing it to the church offering, the third step is impossible to square with the Scriptural tithe: the Israelites were to eat their own tithe at the major feasts in Jerusalem. We don't eat the money that we bring to church! Nor do we have any spiritual need to bring food to the church.

We now know that what happened in the Temple at Jerusalem was a shadow representation of what goes on in God's eternal Temple in Heaven. We know that we must find a spiritual interpretation for the physical events that went on in the earthly Temple. But if we are going to use that principle, then doesn't it also apply to the tithe Law? Can we say with any honesty that everything else about the Temple pointed to spiritual realities but the tithe points to American dollars? And can we be so naïve to think that God has need of our currency in his Temple in Heaven? We have seen that the people brought the fruit of their labor to the Temple worship and ate it there in God's presence, and we are obligated to find the spiritual reality for that in the age of the Church – but our offering plates don't qualify as a spiritual fulfillment!

- **The other laws** – You must also consider the other laws for Temple support. In fact, they were more directly involved in the building's maintenance, supplies, and so forth than the tithe was. Much of what is given in offerings in churches nowadays would fall under these other laws rather than the Law of tithing. But nobody mentions them! They were specific taxes, levied on the Israelites as so much paid per head, and they insured that the Temple services would continue uninterrupted. My point is that, if we are obligated to keep the tithe Law (the purpose of which was not what we use it for now) then why aren't we also obligated to keep the half-shekel tax Law and the valuation tax Law as well – which were more to the purpose for how we use the money in our churches now?

The fact is that modern Christians have borrowed the word "tithe" and applied new meanings to it, creating a lot of confusion in the process. Probably a more consistent example of the Old Testament Laws was the method used during the days of the Puritans. The taxes that citizens in each town paid were used in part for the support of the church – the church's expenses, including the pastor's salary, was paid for out of public tax revenues, not the offering plate. For good or ill, they were more in line with the Old Testament requirements than modern tithing practices. Of course, the political doctrine of the separation of Church and State has made that situation impossible now.

- **Christ's comments** – Christ mentioned tithing a couple of times and shed some additional light on the subject. He rebuked the religious leaders (who faithfully paid their tithe, by the way) because they didn't understand the point of the Law:

> Woe to you, teachers of the Law and Pharisees, you hypocrites! You give a tenth of your spices – mint, dill and cummin. But you have neglected the more important matters of the Law – justice, mercy and faithfulness. You should have practiced the

latter, without neglecting the former. (Matthew 23:23)

Notice first what he calls the act of tithing – a "matter of the Law." That's not to be taken lightly. The Jews indeed were to obey the Law, even down to the little details of tithing all of their income. But that label he attached to tithing should send up warning flags for Christians eager to do whatever they find in the Scriptures. Some matters – especially many things in the Mosaic Law – have been taken care of for us by the only One who can keep the Law perfectly.

Second, he evidently feels that the bare act of tithing won't necessarily please God. We can see this more clearly in another passage:

The Pharisee stood up and prayed about himself; "God, I thank you that I am not like all other men – robbers, evildoers, adulterers – or even like this tax collector. I fast twice a week and give a tenth of all I get" ... I tell you that this man [*that is, the tax collector*], rather than the other [*that is, the Pharisee*], went home justified before God. (Luke 18:11-14)

Tithing in itself doesn't please God, contrary to what we are often told. One can tithe one's income to the last penny and still be on God's bad side. It's too easy to hide behind outward obedience to the Law and not have the inner reality of the Spirit's work of regeneration. But that's a typical shortcoming of the Law – it can't change our hearts to conform to God's will – and that's why the Gospel takes a different approach.

- **The New Testament witness** – There is none. The only other place that the word "tithe" is used in the New Testament is in Hebrews where the author discusses the tithe that Abraham paid to Melchizedek; there his point is most definitely not to show our obligation to tithe our income, but to show the preeminence of Melchizedek and therefore Christ. The rest of the New Testament is completely silent about the subject. If the maintenance of the Church is so dependent on tithes, and if it's true that we are obligated to tithe to keep the Church going, then why don't the Apostles at least mention it? As a matter of fact, they do talk about finances and the Church – which we will look at shortly – but definitely not in terms of tithing.

- **It was the Law** – Aside from all the other arguments about the real meaning of tithing and the existence of the other Laws, the fundamental problem about the Law of tithing is that it's a part of the Mosaic Covenant given at Mt. Sinai – the famous Law which the Israelites were required to obey and which Christ obeyed on behalf of God's people.

    The purpose of the Law was to keep the Israelites in line until a better way of pleasing God could be put into place; Paul describes this in Galatians 3:19-4:7. The Israelites were spiritually immature, in their nursery years, so to speak; the Lord had to use Law to keep them in line. But when Christ came, that way of dealing with the children was set aside; the child grew up, he had the right to claim his inheritance, and he started living by faith instead of by the Law. "Now that faith has come, we are no longer under the supervision of the Law." (Galatians 3:25)

If that's true (and Paul warns that, if anybody teaches anything else, "let him be eternally condemned!" – Galatians 1:8-9) then when someone tries to impose the requirements of the Law on our conscience, the reaction of every good Christian should be to turn his back on it. Not that we are free to sin; far from it. We are called to live by faith in the Son of God now, which will lead us to do far more for the glory of God and holy living than we could ever hope to achieve under the Law's discipline. As we will see below, the Law of the tithe is a poor substitute for what the Lord has called his children to do under the reign of Christ.

- **Does Malachi apply here?** – The passage in Malachi is often used to support tithing in the Church. In fact, it has a challenging side to it: "Test me in this … and see if I will not throw open the floodgates of Heaven and pour out so much blessing that you will not have room enough for it." (Malachi 3:10) You can really motivate people with a challenge like that. If they aren't motivated, they may even be accused of lacking faith in God to provide for their needs.

  First, it's true that we are too often stingy when it comes to supporting the Lord's work, and faith is certainly the answer. But it seems to me that another passage would fit our Christian situation a little better than this one does. These verses in Malachi are, after all, talking about the tithe – the Law that was binding on all the Israelites. They were obligated to pay the tithe; so much so that the Lord called them "robbers" when they didn't. Not paying the tithe meant that they were "law breakers." (James 2:10-11) That's not the situation that we Christians are in.

  Second, if we are obligated to heed the rebuke in Malachi and start paying the tithe, then our duty is to pay the tithe – if we must obey the Law, then we must do exactly what the Law says to do. We can't just borrow the word and do what we like. We must gather a tenth of our income, bring it to the Temple, and there during the religious feasts of the Jewish calendar eat our tithe. Anything short of this will be breaking the requirements of the Law. Note carefully that the text says, "that there may be *food*" – where? "In the *storehouse*." Obviously this has to do with the particular problem of having enough food for the holy days. Why do people ignore what is so obvious here?

Third, I wonder where the rest of the book of Malachi went? The Lord severely chastised the Israelites for many things in this book, not just for neglecting the tithe. Why aren't we Christians told that God is displeased with us for – 1) bringing crippled animals to the sacrifice, (Malachi 1:8), 2) the priests violating the covenant with Levi, (Malachi 2:8), 3) Judah desecrating the sanctuary (Malachi 2:11)? Why is only one of the scathing denunciations of Malachi picked out for us and the rest of them ignored? Why don't we hear sermons on the other requirements as well? I think you can see what I'm getting at.

Someone might say, "But those other points are true for us Christians in a spiritual sense." That's true. We are concerned, for example, that we bring to God an acceptable sacrifice; only with us it isn't animals but our "bodies as living sacrifices, holy and pleasing to God which is your spiritual worship." (Romans 12:1) But that only supports my argument all the more. If all the other points in Malachi are only true of us Christians in a spiritualized sense, why is the Law of tithing any different? Why are we obligated to obey the tithe physically as the Jews did when we are permitted – or required! – to find a spiritual obedience to the other laws? And especially when the Law no longer has power over our conscience, it seems strange that we must follow the literal meaning of the tithe Law when we don't have to for the other Laws. As a matter of fact, I think that there is a spiritual reality for us Christians that the tithe Law was trying to address, which we will get into later.

- **What about the Levites?** – Let's go back to that passage which refers to the Levites – Numbers 18. The advocates of tithing often claim that tithes support the salaries involved in church work;   pastors are like the Levites because they take time which would have ordinarily been given to secular work in order to minister to the saints. That's true, but when we look at the situation of the Levites we discover that the two groups aren't as much alike as we may have thought. In fact, it can be dangerous to draw parallels between the two!

Numbers 18:22 says that the Israelites were not allowed in the Tent of Meeting – later on that included the Temple. The surrounding courts were all right, but inside where the priests ministered to the Lord was forbidden territory to all the tribes of Israel except the Levites. The Levites' special duty was to minister before the Lord on behalf of the rest of Israel.

That just doesn't carry over into our age. Every Christian is not only permitted into the Temple of God in Heaven, but he is *expected* to be there praying and interceding for the saints and claiming the treasures of Heaven. The veil has been torn in two so that "whosoever will" may come straight into the presence of God. The Roman Church still keeps the ordinary layman out in the courtyard of Heaven, and claims that only her priests can go to God for the grace that they need; but the Protestant

Churches have gloried in the fact that every child of God has the right of direct access to the Lord's throne. Because of this, we have all become spiritual Levites – "you have made them to be a Kingdom and priests to serve our God." (Revelation 5:10) We no longer have a special class of men among us.

Pastors and teachers have an entirely different job than the Levites had. The Levites ministered before God; pastors and teachers minister to the saints. The former offered sacrifices; the latter teach the people. Now, it's true that "the worker deserves his wages." (1 Timothy 5:18) But let's not bring out the Law of tithing in order to support the pastor, saying that we are obligated to take care of our Levites. If we followed the letter of the Law as it stands, we should all get paid!

- **Checking the standards** – Traditionally Christians have checked one place to find out if they are obligated to follow a particular teaching: the Gospel of Christ. If it's not something that Christ told them to do, and if it isn't in the teaching of the Apostles as recorded in the Epistles of the New Testament, then don't be surprised if they become wary and start asking questions.

We have been warned by the Apostles, remember, that the Law from Sinai is not the way that we will achieve righteousness and life. Much of it has been taken care of by Christ, which means that now *we* don't have to. Some of it gets worked into our hearts by the special action of the Spirit – but it still isn't *our* own doing. Though the entire Bible is useful for our faith and life (2 Timothy 3:16) we can't use all parts of it in the same way that the early Israelites did. Since we are Christians, we have to start with what makes us *Christian* and see how that

affects our relationship with the rest of the Bible –
especially the Law.

Given that, we can say that tithing is *not* part of the
Gospel. It's part of the Law of Sinai, and therefore we
can assume that our obligation to it is about the same as
many of the other laws that Moses gave the Israelites.
From here we can continue to study the Law and what it
might mean in our life of faith; but I believe that it's safe
to assume that we are not obligated to follow it to the
letter in the way that the Israelites were.

Why churches do it

If you've been following the argument so far, you might be
saying, "Well, you may have a point. But if this is true, why have
churches insisted for so long on the necessity of tithing?" That's
a good question, and there are several reasons we can find for
churches teaching the duty of the tithe:

- **They need the finances**. Almost all churches need money
  to operate. Building costs, rent and maintenance; the
  pastor's salary and whoever else may be on the staff;
  books and supplies; utilities, parking lots, advertisements
  in the paper; moneys sent to missions and conferences and
  so forth; and many other expenses. It takes a pretty
  significant cash flow to keep a system like that running
  year round. So members are usually taught, when they
  join a church, that "you *will* support this church with your
  time and your money!" A tenth is a handy percentage for
  churches to operate under; if everyone gave a tenth of
  their income, a church could meet all of its expenses
  easily.

Sometimes, though, I get the feeling that we've put the
cart before the horse. They hire a pastor, which makes a

certain amount of money necessary for his salary; then they go out and buy a building, which makes another sum of money necessary in order to buy it; and so on through all the rest of the expenses. Then they go to the church members and say "Now you have to come up with this much money in order that the work of God can go on." Well, under those circumstances I agree: a tithe is the *only* way they are going to pay for all of that.

What I *don't* agree with is the necessity of the expenses. You don't need an expensive building to be a church; you don't need to hire a pastor at modern American wages to be a church. A true church is never *more* than the New Testament says it is: a body of believers, each with their own gifts, under the shepherding care of elders and deacons, coming together (it can be out in the fields like so many churches have had to do in history) to encourage each other, to do their duty toward each other, and to worship the Lord. Anything more than that is purely cultural and something we can do without if need be.

So my point is this: church leaders are allowed to ask their members to support the church only in matters that make them a church, as the New Testament defines "church;" they cannot *expect* the members to support a church with twentieth century expenses. They can ask, but they can't demand it (which is the purpose of the Law). And a church member is doing his duty to God and his people when he gives money for what the New Testament says he *must*, not necessarily everything that goes on in a church "program." If everyone there wants padded seats, that's one thing; but to expect Christians to tithe because it's their duty *before God* and then use the money to pad the seats, is being dishonest stewards of the Lord's money.

- **They need some way to enforce giving**. The Law is a wonderful device to make people feel guilty and get them to do what you want them to do. In fact, that's the precise purpose of the Law: to convict of sin. When people hear the Law, they realize that they have broken it, and they will often do something to make up for it – especially if you are there ready to suggest the kind of penance they can do. When a preacher declares that "You have robbed God!" that will almost always bring the people to their knees in troubled spirit; when he offers them a way out with "bring your whole tithe into the storehouse" then they will immediately dig into their pockets. That makes them feel better.

Because the modern church has such pressing and continuous financial needs, church leaders are concerned that the money *keeps on coming in*. If contributions drop then they get alarmed, and rightly so; if there isn't enough money then their church isn't going to work. The modern church is run much like a business: there are set expenses, and there has to be a certain level of cash flow if they are going to keep the doors open. I'm sorry if this sounds crass, but denominational headquarters will often close up new churches because they didn't achieve a predetermined income after the first or second year; it often has nothing to do with the quality of spiritual work going on there.

In light of this reality of the modern world, the tithe is a handy way of holding the members feet to the fire. Look here, they say, you see the expenses that are involved in running the Lord's work. If you don't do your fair share then it will fail – you don't want *that* on your conscience, do you? If you pay your tithe then you will fulfill your obligation to the Lord's work.

Well, stating the problem like this shows up its weaknesses. First of all, a church is not judged by its income. A church can be a vital church even if it fails miserably in its finances. An abundance of money is not a good indicator of spirituality. Second, we've already seen that many of the expenses of today's churches aren't things that the Bible demands a church to incur in the Lord's Name, and may be unfair burdens on church members. We just may have to learn to tighten our belts: if there isn't money enough to do what we want, and if we can't find anything in the Bible that supports what we want money for, then we will have to drop the idea. That's far better than doing it anyway and demanding in the Lord's Name that members pick up the tab!

- **They fail to see the tithe as part of the Law**. I'm convinced that many church leaders are not guilty of maliciously burdening people's hearts with the Mosaic Law. They claim to be Gospel preachers and I believe them. The problem is that they haven't studied the tithe Law very much, and they aren't fully aware of all the Biblical requirements involved in tithing. That's why we've taken so much time in this study to explore the Law. Which leads to the next point.

- **They lack faith**. Because the needs are so great, and they don't appreciate the fact that tithing is the Mosaic Law in all of its Old Testament severity and powerlessness to save, and they think that the church won't survive unless something like tithing is imposed on the members, the church leaders turn to tithing. You see? It's a panic solution instead of a solution of faith. Instead of doing it God's way (which we'll look at in a minute) they turn to the security and outward comfort of the Law.

The Lord's solution for the survival of the Church is *not* the Law, I can assure you. Israel failed to keep the Law, and Christ didn't come to try that method again on the Church. This time he is using the Spirit to put the rewards and results of his righteousness in our hearts. Instead of following the Law, we follow Christ; instead of our own works of obedience, it's the Spirit's work in us that saves us; instead of obedience to the Law, it's now faith in Christ.

Though every good Christian agrees with that, it's difficult to live it. In the case of the financial dealings in a church, the Apostles have clearly laid out our obligations – but doing it their way doesn't sound at all businesslike! How can a church survive if it does it *exactly* like the New Testament describes? How can we be certain that the Spirit will guide the affairs of the church to success using *his* methods? The Law sounds much more reasonable and workable. So instead of having the faith necessary to trust God to know what he is doing, we back up to the immature measures of the time of the Israelites.

Why tithing won't work

The tithe will never work. For one thing, it's not God's way of doing things – not in the Church at any rate. You will find as you study the Scriptures that God has certain *ways* of doing things; sometimes he changes methods depending on who he's working with, but his ways always work and are calculated to bring about his desired purposes. One of the most pointed Scriptures in the Bible refers to people not knowing how God does things, and what that will mean in their relationship to him:

That is why I was angry with that generation, and I said, "Their hearts are always going astray, *and they have not known my ways.*" So I declared on oath in my anger, "they shall never enter my rest." (Hebrews 3:10-11)

Obviously it's very important to find out *how* God wants to do things; we can't be sloppy about work in the church and expect him to bless our actions that he didn't require of us.

Another reason that tithing won't work is because not everyone in the church is going to tithe anyway. The leaders can put on the pressure and plead and make people feel guilty all they want and still only get some of the members to go along with tithing. What about those who won't? How do you explain their behavior to the rest of the church? If you're not really the legalistic type, you're going to have a problem keeping the pressure up on the tithers while, at the same time, admitting that the non-tithers aren't obligated to keep the Law. On the other hand, if you are partial to the Law then you are going to be in the unenviable position of siding with the Law against your Christian brothers. We see an example of that in Galatians when Peter, siding with the Law group of believers, separated himself from the Gentiles who weren't following the Law. Paul blasted him for an attitude like that. (Galatians 2: 16)

There are several other important reasons why tithing just won't work in the Church:

- **It doesn't match the New Testament situation**. The very nature of the old Israelite situation doesn't match the situation that we find ourselves in now. The Temple, with all its sacrifices and ceremonies, was a shadow of the reality to come in Christ and the Church. As Hebrews teaches us, the Israelites had to offer their sacrifices over and over again because the blood of bulls and goats simply can't take away one's sin. (Hebrews 9:9) The tithe Law was closely bound up with this sacrificial system – a system that God set aside when the real solution appeared in Christ.

The people went several times a year to the Temple at Jerusalem for special feasts and holy days, and sometimes those occasions extended over the entire week. Those sacrifices were important, and it was important that the people come to the Temple for the ceremony – they weren't allowed to stay home. They had to eat something while they were there, of course, which is where the tithe came into the picture. It all boils down to this: tithing only makes sense in that situation, when the Jews came to Jerusalem to offer their sacrifices.

Now in our day we also have a Temple, but it's in Heaven. (Hebrews 9:11) One sacrifice has been offered there, and no more will be offered there again. Anything from earth that we might want to bring to that Temple is pretty useless in Heaven, since the Father is only pleased with the sacrifice of Christ and what he provides for us. So tithing doesn't fit anywhere in this picture for us Christians. It's a physical shadow that just won't carry over into our modern circumstances.

- **It's not the Spirit's way**. A door is a good picture of how to enter the Kingdom of God. If you want to go through the doorway, you have to turn the knob first. If the Jews wanted to enter into the Kingdom of God then the "knob" they had to turn was obedience to the Law. We Christians also want to get into the Kingdom of God, but our "knob" is faith in Christ. The goal is the same, but the means to the end is entirely different. (We could get into a discussion of the Old Testament saints who had a saving faith, and who were included in the Church of God because of their faith in Christ – what the Spirit enabled them to see of him; but that, after all, as Paul tells us in

Romans and elsewhere, was the real spiritual goal of the physical symbolisms of their day. It doesn't lessen the sharp terrors of the legal system; the Jews were *required* to follow the Law to the letter, even if the Lord accepted some of them on the basis of faith in the Messiah.)

Paul talks about the difference between obedience to Law and living by faith. "But if you are led by the Spirit, you are not under Law." (Galatians 5 18) If you have to be told to do something before you'll do anything, then we'll have to write up hundreds or thousands of laws for you because there are a lot of things that you must do to be acceptable to God and man. Then you must be sure that you understand all those laws – all the possible applications that you may be expected to use. And you'll have to continually check your performance to see if you are actually doing what the Law requires of you; you mustn't leave anything undone. You see? Living by the Law is an overwhelming task that no living human has ever achieved – except for Christ.

But if you live by the Spirit, all you have to do is follow him wherever he leads. Christ has already made you acceptable to God and man, and now all that remains is for you to go where the Spirit leads, and do what the Spirit tells you to do, as he works the righteousness of Christ out in your life. So, much of the Law is already behind you – Christ took care of it for you. And what is left of the Law will be perfectly satisfied with your behavior because the Spirit prompts and strengthens you to do and say the right thing – again, something that you can't take any credit for.

All that is to say that the Law of tithing has been and will be taken care of – but not by you. Your duty is to keep your eyes on Christ, and listen to his Spirit as he leads you; you are not to focus on the Law, which you can't satisfy anyway.

- **Christ won't be behind it**. The Lord Jesus was a very particular man. What he was in favor of, he really liked; but what he didn't like, you weren't going to change his mind about it.

For one thing, if you really think that you need to keep the Law, then he thinks that you need to keep it to the letter. "Anyone who breaks one of the least of these commandments ..." (Matthew 5:19) "Unless your righteousness surpasses that of the Pharisees ..." (Matthew 5:20) "You should have practiced the latter without leaving the former undone." (Luke 11:42) "You still lack one thing." (Luke 18:22). If you're aiming for the Law then you'd better aim high, if you hope to get Christ's approval. He knows what it takes to satisfy the Law to its fullest extent.

Second, he specifically told us that he himself has taken on the job of fulfilling the requirements of the Law. "Do not think that I have come to abolish the Law or the Prophets; I have not come to abolish them but to fulfill them." (Matthew 5:17) Now if he has taken care of the Law, what are we doing going back to it? Isn't that what Paul warned against in Galatians? And Hebrews 6 and 10 puts turning away from Christ for *whatever reason* (including returning to the Law) on the level of an insult.

Third, tithing (or *anything* in the Law) isn't the tool that Christ has chosen to build his Church. In the old days, Moses (and the Law which he brought to Israel) was the overseer of the people of God, and his ways (i.e., the Law) was the rule by which the house of God operated. But now one greater than Moses is here. "Jesus has been found worthy of greater honor than Moses, just as the builder of a house has greater honor than the house itself." (Hebrews 3:3) And when he came to take over his house, he brought his own collection of tools to build it up – not the same set that Moses used. Tithing addresses the physical needs of the Temple, but the Church has something much greater at stake than that – so it needs a special set of tools and materials for its construction.

- **It takes away from Christian responsibility**. It's a common ailment of human nature that people won't do any more than they have to do. The Law might work as far as it goes, but you never know if people really *want* to do it if they're being told that they *have* to do it. More often than not they will grudgingly obey, and they will quit obeying if the Law is ever relaxed. Also, they feel that they have done their duty if they obeyed the letter of the Law; they don't want to hear about any *further* responsibilities.

Children are often like that. They only do their chores because their parents tell them to, threatening some punishment if they don't and a reward if they do. What they don't understand is that doing the chores makes home life so much better; but then they probably won't see that until they grow up and have their own responsibilities.

Christians are often like that too. For some reason they are happiest when someone hangs the letter of the Law over their heads and either threatens God's displeasure or promises God's approval. They will do no more than what is absolutely required of them. Then they think that they've done their duty and will refuse to go the extra mile that faith calls them to. Jesus gave an excellent example of the two kinds of religious people in the story of the good Samaritan – the legalists who hid behind their duties, and the faithful few who rolled up their sleeves and did what was necessary, not simply what was required by Law.

If a minister or teacher teaches that Christians are duty-bound to pay the tithe in order to please God, because the Word instructs them to do so, what they are really doing is this: they are misleading the people from their real duty before God. They will pay the tithe, as required, thinking that they've done their job, when in reality they haven't even started on the tremendous spiritual job that lies around them. The ultimate effect of Law-preaching is to kill the desire for Gospel duty.

If people would start feeling responsible for one another, instead of hiding behind the minimum requirements that they do for show ("Sorry, I gave at the office!") there wouldn't be any more talk about tithing, because tithing is a poor reflection of the potential for good that exists in the Church. If Christians grew up spiritually, they would see for themselves the problems and solutions around them and start taking some action, instead of primly dropping some money in the plate and turning their backs on the real needs facing them. Responsibility takes over when the Law is powerless to do any more.

- **We never do what the Law says anyway**. We referred to this before but it bears repeating. It's not much use to obey the Law unless we intend to do exactly what it says. We've seen that the Law of tithing was very specific: one had to gather together a tenth of one's income, in whatever form, take it to the Temple and store it, and then eat it during the religious feasts in Jerusalem. I personally don't know anybody who does that, though I know of many who insist on "tithing" their income.

105

If we aren't going to do what the Law says, then our "tithing" isn't going to do any good, least of all satisfy the Law's requirements. We're focusing our attention and energies on something that we were mistaken about, something that won't do anything for us. If a man dug a hole in the ground only to find that it was the wrong spot to dig in, what has he achieved for all his efforts? If a Christian tithes his income simply because the Law says to, what has he gained spiritually? Has he done anything for Christ's Church? Especially if the Lord wanted him to use that money for other things! And as we will see, the Lord has many things in mind for our money.

What churches ought to do

After looking at the subject carefully, it appears that tithing is for the Old Testament times and not for the times of the New Testament Church. But we can't stop here, because there may be some who feel that we are throwing out the baby with the bath water. If we aren't going to rely on the Law of tithing to support the physical needs of the Church, then what are we going to rely on? There *are* physical needs, and individual Christians are responsible somehow to meet those needs. It's not good enough to give them a law to live by, though, simply because they won't obey the law to God's satisfaction and the Law isn't enough to meet the situation at hand. So how are we going to approach this? Is there really a New Testament solution?

There is, but it's based on faith – a much tougher thing, it seems, for people to live by than the Law. In fact, faith in Christ is something that God has to give us if we are going to do it at all. We often talk about faith, and we hope we have some. But when the difficult situations in life threaten to overwhelm us, we will see if we have faith or not. Faith is for those times when nothing else under the sun is going to get the job done – the Law can't do a satisfactory job, let alone our own futile efforts.

The most important fact that we have to believe is this: Christ is working in his Church. It's too easy to forget about him when we get wrapped up in church leaders and church programs and buildings and money – all the works of men. What really makes a church, however, is the spiritual stonework that the master Builder is putting together. It's a building that "cannot be shaken" (Hebrews 12:27) because he makes it out of redeemed souls who will live forever. It's a home for God (1 Corinthians 3:16), who can't live in a physical temple (2 Chronicles 6:18) but who will live among his people forever. And he connects those stones with bonds that can't break – the fruit of the Spirit – with a skill that defies human understanding. None of us will ever know the full extent of his labors until we get to Heaven and see the work he has done among us.

In one sense his work is highly visible. He told us that "a tree is recognized by its fruit" (Matthew 12:33) – meaning that there are unmistakable signs of his handiwork that we should be able to see. If a person is a new creation then he will live like it; Christ doesn't make him a Christian just so he can continue to look and live like a pagan. And his work in the Church is equally visible. Paul tells us what should be happening in a church if the Spirit is really at work there: all the parts helping and supporting each other, coming together in unity (thus proving that it really is one body), replacing the old sins which hurt each other with new graces which strengthen each other. (1 Corinthians 12, Galatians 5: 26) And when Christ reigns supreme in a church, molding and making it into his image, the world will be convicted by the sight and perhaps themselves come to the knowledge of God. (1 Peter 2:12)

But in another sense the work of Christ in a church isn't a visible thing at all. For the last two thousand years, people have tried to make the Church a matter of buildings and dress and outward ceremonies and all kinds of material things. It isn't. In fact, it's spiritually dangerous to equate the Church with anything that is part of *this* world because the Church is eternal, a work of God that will never die, based on the never-ending life of Christ himself, whereas everything in this world is destined to be destroyed. We can't go back to the situation that the Jews were in: their temple was made out of stone, ours is made out of the "living stones" of God's people; their land of promise was Palestine, ours is Heaven; their sacrifice was bulls and goats, ours is the Son of God. Theirs was a visible reality, ours is an invisible one. (1 Corinthians 15:35-55)

Since this is true, we of the Church will have to approach the matter of money and possessions in a different way than through Old Testament Law. Our situation is different now, especially in these ways:

• **The Temple is spiritual**. This is the most important point to get a hold of. In the Old Testament the Temple was a physical building in Jerusalem, to which the Jews came from all around Israel for their seasons of worship and sacrifice. But our Temple is not a physical building, and it isn't located anywhere on earth. The sacrifices there are done – made once by Christ, and nobody needs to make any more.

   Everything that happened in the Temple in Jerusalem was a "shadow" – a physical representation of the spiritual reality yet to be revealed. So the Lord never intended the Israelites to get sidetracked on those physical issues; he expected them to have the faith to see through to the Kingdom of God behind it all.

   Now, in the Church, we have supposedly dispensed with all those shadows and we don't need crutches for our faith anymore. Although we meet in a building, we know that the physical building is not the Church. We know that Christ's sacrifice has taken care of our sin, and we don't need to take care of it ourselves. We also know that taxation – the tithe and valuation laws – won't help promote our worship in Christ the least bit, though it was critical to the Old Testament Temple economy.

- **The Spirit moves God's people**. The Jews were pushed from behind by the Law. The Law pointed out sin, hedged a person around with its protection, and punished law-breakers. But that's not how things are done in our Christian era. We don't (or shouldn't have to!) need pushing to do the will of God; we are "compelled" by the love of God – if you want to call that "pushing." (2 Corinthians 5:14) Instead of a servile fear of punishment, we live by love – toward God and man – and look for ways to serve both. (1 Peter 5:2)

In the days of the Israelites the Lord used the Law to make sure his will got done. How else could he manage such a rebellious lot? They had the same kind of heart that their pagan neighbors had, unfortunately, and the Law served the necessary function of keeping them in control.

But Christians don't live by servile fear. We know that which the Israelites seemed to be ignorant of: the real purpose of the Law is to describe the perfect man, a person who lives a holy life simply because he wants to. Whatever he does is good. His character is impeccable. He leaves no good thing undone, and he does no bad thing.

If man's heart was unstained and completely free from sin and the desire to sin, then the Law would have no problem with him. But there was only one perfect man with whom the Law had no argument. Does this mean that the rest of us have no hope? Is the Law always going to be a terror for us? Not with the Spirit in our hearts! He "compels" us, moves us, to "will and to act according to his good purpose." How the Spirit makes us do the perfect will of God and it still be true that we truly *want* to do God's will – in other words, we do it because we want to, and yet the Spirit makes us do it (Philippians 2:13) – is a mystery none of us can solve. But the fact is that a Christian doesn't need the Law to tell him what to do, and he isn't worried by its terrors. He will know what each situation of his life requires, and (if he is following the Spirit) he will do what pleases God his Father.

Does the New Testament discuss the use of money in the Church? Let's look at some passages and then draw some conclusions from them:

The Church in Acts – The birth of the Church was a tremendous event, and the kinds of things that happened then were so startlingly different from the previous centuries of Jewish worship and life that it really is a breath of "new life" in the story of the Bible. But for the same reason – its startling reality and vitality – people have often thought that it was never going to happen in history again. They think that it was a unique event; it happened once and will never be repeated. The "Apostolic" church is a goal that we should try to aim for (and even that is more than some people will admit to nowadays!); but we will never reach it, practically speaking.

I disagree. If we have trouble reaching the goal that the first church set for us, it's probably because we want too many of our own goals too and both of them together won't work. I believe that the Apostolic

110

church was an *example*, not an unattainable goal, for the rest of the Church.

One thing that they did was to share their possessions. "All the believers were together and had everything in common. Selling their possessions and goods, they gave to anyone as he had need." (Acts 2:44-45) That idea gives modern Americans the chills. Give up my hard-earned possessions, my comforts, for someone who most likely doesn't deserve it? We therefore say that, probably, such things happened once in a while, under great need, but surely they weren't a common occurrence! Not so! Read this:

All the believers were one in heart and mind. No one claimed that any of his possessions was his own, but they shared everything they had ... There were no needy persons among them. For from time to time those who owned land or houses sold them, brought the money from the sales and put it at the Apostles' feet, and it was distributed to anyone as he had need. (Acts 4:32, 34-35)

Now just so we don't miss the point, we ought to make a list of the things that we bring money to church for, in a column on one side of the paper; then, referring to these passages from Acts, list what the early Christians brought money to church for. I think a fair examination will end up with two completely different lists. It seems that we don't have the same priorities that they had. Oftentimes church members will claim that "I didn't know that so-and-so needed help!" No wonder – churches aren't often geared around finding those needs and meeting them as its number one priority.

Can anybody find fault with the early Christians for not "tithing" and giving money for a building and salaries for the hired help? None of them were concerned about tithing; what they were concerned about were these brothers and sisters who were in need. Was their love for each other good enough to satisfy the Law? "Love is the fulfillment of the Law." (Romans 13:10) In other words, because of *love* (not Law), nobody went without the necessities of life.

Worthy workers – Paul tells us that certain people in the church deserve some monetary reward for their time and efforts.

> The elders who direct the affairs of the church well are worthy of double honor, especially those whose work is preaching and teaching. For the Scripture says, "Do not muzzle the ox while it is treading out the grain," and "The worker deserves his wages." (1 Timothy 5:17-18)

It's interesting, isn't it, that he didn't go to the Levite passages to support his argument! Supporting the workers in the church isn't a matter of taxation (tithing) or even obligation per se, but a matter of "honor" and what seems right. The reason he puts it like this is because he's talking to Christians – hopefully mature Christians – who understand what it means to do what is fair and right of their own accord. (He took the same approach with Philemon.)

Second, notice he says that the "elders" are worthy of honor, including teaching and non-teaching elders. He makes no distinction. It's our distinction when we limit financial reward to a hired "expert" who comes in from outside to do a job that none of *us* want to do.

Most people would shut this argument down right here, arguing that such a thing wouldn't be feasible for the ordinary church. My response is that people can do whatever they like, but Paul tells us here what is right and "honorable" for a church to do.

Elders, if they are doing their job as the Lord expects of them, take a lot of time and trouble to "feed" the sheep. It involves long hours of agonizing on their knees before God over the people's spiritual needs, counseling, living exemplary lives, studying the Word and teaching those truths that will benefit the people, and much more. They deserve some sort of recognition for their hard work and spiritual skill, and several passages show us the pressure they are under to build the house of God skillfully – Hebrews 13:17; 1 Peter 5:1-4; James 3:1. Rewarding only the person who was hired for the primary spot in the church's hierarchy is completely sidestepping this issue of publicly recognizing all who work in the Lord's vineyard.

<u>Jesus' comments</u> – Jesus made some interesting comments about Christians and their money. Although we can't really say whether he meant to address the use of church finances, we can nevertheless learn about the individual Christian's priorities – and from that, what he will end up doing in the church setting.

> I tell you, use worldly wealth to gain friends for yourselves, so that when it is gone, you will be welcomed into eternal dwellings. (Luke 16:9)

Isn't this a puzzling statement? What does he mean to "gain friends" with one's wealth? I believe that we saw an example of it in Acts 2:42-47. Give it away, he is telling us. Notice he said, "When it is gone ..."

Something isn't gone unless we gave it away to begin with. And the context here is the parable of the shrewd manager who gave away his master's wealth to people who owed his master something; he touched their needs, in other words. We may not know what this will mean in our own lives, but the principle is unmistakable. It's also clear that this is not what we usually go to church for.

> You still lack one thing. Sell everything you have and give to the poor, and you will have treasure in Heaven. Then come, follow me. (Luke 18:22)

The usual interpretation of this story is that Jesus put his finger on the besetting sin of this rich man: he loved his money too much to give it up. I agree – and he says the same to anybody else who doesn't have it in his heart to "give to the poor" and follow him. Isn't it comfortable to drop a ten-dollar bill in the offering plate without anybody demanding more of us? Even giving a tithe is better than having to find out what the needs are in the congregation and then doing whatever it takes to meet those needs. Every Christian should be sensitive to this; but shouldn't the structure of the church itself help to promote those kinds of activities, instead of putting a plate under everyone's nose and whisking the offering away to promote "God's work" in some general sense that nobody ever sees?

This man may have thought that he satisfied the Law's demands in every other area, but Jesus pointed out that the Law isn't satisfied yet – not by a long shot. It takes more than just obedience to make Jesus pleased with us. Follow the Ten Commandments?

Tithe all of your income? You still aren't acceptable. You must do more, much more than the Law requires (which is, after all, only the minimum.) You must love your neighbor in a way that will help him.

Partnership – Paul never begged for money. He learned how to live with plenty and with need, because he depended solely on the Lord to provide for him. That's faith. Ministries that depend solely on pleading for money to finance their operations (even though they "pray" for God's blessing) are sidestepping faith and doing things their own way, a way that seems much more reasonable than God's way.

But since the Spirit moves Christians to do God's will, sometimes a few mature Christians would save up some money and send it along to Paul. The Philippian church was like this. Of course Paul knew who was responsible for this gracious act – he thanked God first – but he also knew that the Philippians had their priorities straight.

I thank my God every time I remember you. In all my prayers for all of you, I always pray with joy because of your partnership in the gospel from the first day until now, being confident of this, that he who began a good work in you will carry it on to completion until the day of Christ Jesus. (Philippians 1:3-6)

It seems that this was a rare grace among churches, even in the days of the "Apostolic church."

In the early days of your acquaintance with the gospel, when I set out from Macedonia, not one church shared with me in the matter of giving and receiving, except you only; for even when I was in Thessalonica, you sent me aid again and again when I was in need. (Philippians 4:15-16)

It takes some maturity to dig deeply into one's pockets and take care of the needs of the Lord's workers. The immature will give what the Law demands and no more, and they won't go out of their way to find out where the Lord wants the money used.

Another principle of faith is this: Paul never asked anybody to help him. "Not that I am looking for a gift, but I am looking for what may be credited to your account." (Philippians 4:17) Now here is faith on two levels: Paul trusted God, not man, to supply his wants. He never backed down from that position of faith. If people didn't send him something to live on then he was "in need," he was "hungry," he was "in want," and yet he was "content" through it all. (Philippians 4:11-12) Most preachers that I know would find other work if they lost their sizable modern incomes and all the benefits.

The second level is the faith of the Philippians themselves. Paul says that he is looking for something to "credit to their account." Does that remind you of anything?

And he credited it to him as righteousness. (Genesis 15:6)

What caused God to credit righteousness to Abraham? His faith! The faith of the Philippians, their willingness to take God's work seriously and do whatever necessary to further its advance, led them to Paul and his needs. Now this sounds like a simple thing to do, but evidently it was something that most churches in Paul's day just couldn't see. Only the Philippians had the faith to do God's will with their money, even though Paul's needs were obvious to many other churches.

Immature Corinthians – One of the responsibilities of Christians is to support those who labor for the Gospel. Now the only names given to these laborers in the Bible are two: "elders" (I Timothy 5:17), and "those who preach the gospel." (1 Corinthians 9:14) If you study these two passages you will find that it wasn't the *office* that was paid, but the *function* – what that means in our day is that the person who preaches and teaches the Gospel in the church, taking time out from a busy schedule in order to do so, or even devoting his full time to the effort, deserves some financial reward. This is what he does among us, so we will reward him for it.

Don't misunderstand me – the office is important too. A man is called an "elder" because the church recognizes the Spirit's anointing of authority and gifts upon him. That's why they consent to his ministry. But my point is this: it was *what he was doing*, not his position in the church, that deserved compensation. He worked hard for their sake. Our situation is considerably different, however; we hire someone to fill an office and then expect him to produce. We pay him *to work*, instead of paying him *because* he works. Our "pastors" are hired; elders from Christ work regardless of pay. It looks like a fine distinction but actually it makes a great deal of difference in how things get done in the church.

The Corinthians never got the point. Evidently they did only what they were required to do (if that) and they never felt the responsibility to do what they ought to have done. Paul spent a long period of time working with them, bringing them to faith and life, and never asked for the smallest amount of money from them – even though he had the right to ask them! (1 Corinthians 9:18) Now if they would have hired Paul to be their personal "minister" I'm sure they would have agreed on a salary and given him a paycheck every Sunday for his "services". That's immaturity. But since he did it on his own, not making it into a professional "job" but a labor of love that the Lord constrained him to do, he didn't even get so much as a "Thank you." They probably would have paid the office, but it never occurred to them to pay for the labor (especially in light of the fact that he already had a means of supporting himself). He was just another traveling teacher, like many others in those days, and there didn't seem to be any reason to pay him for his labors among them – any more than we would pay an energetic Christian who moves into our community and helps out with the work in a local church.

A brother in need – Probably the most pointed remarks about how Christians should be using their wealth in the church is found in the book of James. In the first place, he sets the stage by describing the true conditions of the poor and the rich in the church. The brother in humble circumstances ought to take pride in his high position. But the one who is rich should take pride in his low position, because he will pass away like a wild flower. (James 1:9-10)

Now that isn't poetry; he meant every word. For two chapters he discusses why God is so much more

118

pleased with the poorer saints than he is with the rich ones.

Then he gets down to the nitty-gritty:

What good is it, my brothers, if a man claims to have faith but has no deeds? Can such faith save him? Suppose a brother or sister is without clothes and daily food. If one of you says to him, "Go, I wish you well; keep warm and well fed," but does nothing about his physical needs, what good is it? In the same way, faith by itself, if it is not accompanied by action, is dead. (James 2:14-17)

This is the kind of thing that motivated the early church to sell their possessions and share their wealth with each other. There will always be those in need in the family of God. You will see them in your church too, if the ministry is holding out the Word of Life to "whosoever will come." The top priority in every church should be this principle:

Religion that God our Father accepts as pure and faultless is this: to look after orphans and widows in their distress and to keep oneself from being polluted by the world. (James 1:27)

The Lord wants to see good doctrine in your church, and a faithful ministry, and praying saints, and regular attendance at the services, and so on. But – as this verse plainly says – he wants to see above all else the saints using money on his special projects instead of lining their own nests. Do the rest, he says, but if you don't do this then all your other religion isn't worth a thing.

Conclusion

Now the purpose of all of this isn't to tear every church down and rebuild it from scratch. Much of what goes on in many evangelical churches will fit into the picture here, in some way, without calling the lie to everything. What I am after is a mature consideration of one's responsibilities to God and man instead of a slavish adherence to Law. The New Testament describes situations where Christians successfully and unsuccessfully struggled to take their new-found responsibilities in Christ seriously. It was a break from the Law, leaving the old system where one only had to pay one's taxes to get God off their back; it was a new world where Christians found themselves responsible to help cure the ills of mankind. The Law wasn't enough to meet the situation.

We haven't discussed many important issues – the purposes and methods that God has for the Church. But we had to look a little at the financial matters of the Church in order to show how the Law of taxation – tithing – is totally inappropriate for the situation of the Church. And we had to discuss some of the purposes and methods of the ministry of Christianity because many churches aren't exactly in line with the New Testament example; they don't seem to be interested in doing what the Apostles were interested in doing. If we can get it straight what we are supposed to be doing, then we won't be misled about matters of the Law.

If we take these New Testament ideas seriously, what will we do in tough situations? For example, if we pinpoint a particular need in the work of the church but the Christians don't rise to the occasion and pay for it, what are we to do? Go back to preaching on the duty of tithing? There are two suggestions for a situation like this:

- **First**, it may not be something that the Lord wants done. We hate to admit things like this, especially when they are our own pet projects. We tend to justify what we want by attaching God's Name to it and finding Scripture to prove its necessity. But often the Spirit will overrule (not always – many times people *do* get their money for their pet projects, but it wasn't any of God's doing; so they will eventually fail) and through the indifference of the people of God put a stop to the project. A wise leader will be able to discern the Spirit's leading and drop the whole thing.

- **Second**, you may be working with immature Christians who don't understand their responsibility before God. This is often true as well. But you have no other options except to remind them from Scripture of their obligations to the Lord's work and then pray for God to do his will in the situation. It's your duty to remind the people of their responsibility; but it isn't your place to beat them over the head for it. They belong to Christ, not you, and *he* is the Lord of his Church – he will lead it as he pleases. You may be upset about how someone else's wife acts in public but it's not *your* place to set her straight; in the same way, the people of God belong to Christ and he reserves the right to discipline his people. Your job is to be the messenger, not the husband himself.

In case these options look unreasonable, like they will never be practical, and if we follow such advice then the church will fail, let me remind you that this is the way Paul handled all his situations that concerned money and churches. We would do well to take his example and trust God to work everything out according to his will. Our ways will never work in the end, no matter how sensible they sound; God's ways always work out in the end, no matter how unreasonable they sound.

Christians and Tithing

Why Creation is a matter of Faith

Why Creation is a matter of faith

The subject of Creation is a shibboleth in our day. If you take seriously the Biblical account, in any way at all, you are branded an anti-scientific obscurantist by the unbelieving camp; and if you hold to the idea of evolution then you are naturally suspect in the Christian camp. There are, of course, all shades of doctrine between total atheism and blind faith. Probably no other doctrine is so much discussed in the public forum today, and the fierce debates in our schools have largely been responsible for its visibility.

The really unfortunate aspect of all of this is that the Christian camp is itself divided on the issue. Christian belief runs from evolution on the one hand to the 6 day, 6000-year-old-earth doctrine on the other. It's a source of great frustration that we can't agree among ourselves about it; there is no way that we can present a united front to the enemies of the Gospel when we are fighting among ourselves.

There is no need to fight among ourselves, however. The Bible holds the clues to the problem; if we can understand its words of mystery and put down our swords long enough to be convinced of its truth, we may find ourselves on the same side after all. It may sound impossible, but the Bible does in fact answer the puzzling question of Creation. We just have to fall back on our distinctives as Christians in order to grasp the point. I can't help it if the unbelievers remain unconvinced, and I'm not surprised that they do; they dance to a different drumbeat than we do and they have no regard for what we count precious. But I do think that Christians should be able to hear the voice of the Spirit of God as he teaches the truth from God's perspective.

Why Creation is an important subject

We aren't dealing with an unimportant issue here; Creation is a fundamental point in our faith. We have got to win this one or we'll lose the war. Creation is one of the most important issues that the Church has to deal with in our generation. The unbelievers know very well that if they can win the battle of how the universe was formed then they have us by the throats; nobody will take the rest of the Bible seriously if the first story in it isn't true.

Your view on Creation will reveal who you think God is and what you think he does in this world. Atheists don't believe in God, and so they think that the universe takes care of itself in a very impersonal way. How did everything in the world get here? What keeps it going? They, of course, think that matter and energy just exist (they don't know how) and they don't think it is a useful question to go any further behind existence; that's a question for the speculations of philosophers. *There is no meaning to anything.* Meaning is simply something that we assign to things; we are the gods who arrange our world to suit our purposes. The earth and the universe are collections of impersonal matter that simply exist, and it is up to us to create whatever we want out of it. This also means, of course, that we can change the rules whenever we want, since rules are entirely man-made. Even the rules themselves are arbitrary, though; the only thing that we can definitely say is that matter exists and events happen – nothing more.

Most unbelievers wouldn't like to carry their theory to the limits because it would mean the utter disintegration of society; how can one believe that there is no ultimate meaning to existence and still carry on a meaningful life? But occasionally one or two of them will admit where their system is taking them – as one letter writer to a science magazine did once. He was offended by the magazine's use of the words "design" and "purpose" when talking of evolution; he very properly (according to the God-less world-view) stated that "Natural selection is, by definition, not directed toward or influenced in its progression by purpose. Whenever one of your articles implies, suggests or states that a trait was developed to do such and such ... it assumes an anti-Darwinian, anti-natural selection posture, promoting myth as scientific fact. While the trait may well serve the function in question, it was neither designed to do so nor did it evolve to do so." (letter to *Science News*, Nov. 3, 1990, p. 275). This is the atheistic position, pure and simple; words like "purpose" and "meaning" and "usefulness" are offensive because they are *not true*.

A Christian, however, challenges that whole viewpoint with the existence of God. If God exists, we say, then we have an answer for your dilemma of meaning. He gives meaning to everything by the design he builds into it and the purposes that he has for everything. We can talk about something "serving its purpose", or "admirably suited for such a purpose", because the Lord made it with purpose and usefulness.

This world has a bridge with the supernatural; God is intimately connected with the world and we can't talk of one without also talking of the other. The things that we see in the world don't make any sense apart from God's direct involvement. He created it, he takes care of it, he commands it and expects acceptable results from it. We literally depend on him for everything we need. And there is one set of unchanging rules that we are all subject to – God's rules. Rather than serving a capricious set of rules made by an ever-changing nature or man's whims, the world serves God and therefore lies under responsibility to him.

We can talk about success or failure now – this is called "judgment" when God looks to see whether we fulfilled our intended purpose. We can talk about value – how much worth something or someone has in God's eyes, and how valuable they are to others who are in need of their skills and characteristics. If something hasn't measured up to the goal that God set for it, then out the window it goes! If it is of no value to the kingdom then it is "thrown out and trampled by men" (Matthew 5:13) as something worthless. But if it proves its value in carrying out the Master's orders, then it will be lifted up and sanctified. This all applies to men as well as to inanimate matter.

In fact, by believing that God created the world we can explain the whole range of human existence as we know it – we can give meaning to the terms and categories that we normally use for life, whereas atheists can't justifiably use those terms. Christians can talk about "serving a purpose" or "the meaning of life" or "usefulness" or "right and wrong" because our system has all that built into it; we can take the world as it stands and explain it, whereas the unbeliever has to deny what he sees and what he knows is the truth in order to hold on to his false system of a world without God. If an unbeliever ever does speak of the world and himself in terms of meaning and purpose and design, he is simply being dishonest with himself and stealing those ideas from the camp of the Christians. He has to; Christians are the only ones who can live responsibly in this world and be at peace with it.

Science's premise

Science operates on a fundamental principle when it studies the world, which is this: *everything is ultimately explainable*. Scientists feel sure that their description of the world, in so far as they have carried it, is true and dependable. The things that they don't have an explanation for yet, well, that will come in time. There is no such thing, as far as they are concerned, as a reality that man cannot understand.

They have a reason for this attitude. If they admit that there are things that are beyond man's ability to comprehend then they are handing those things over to the Church to explain, and they just can't tolerate that thought! Man is no more than a product of the physical universe – but at least he is that, and supposedly capable of understanding the universe because he is one with it. To the scientist, such things as ultimate morality and angels and souls and heaven and hell would upset the picture. Let the old women in the churches deal with such matters, they say; what we want to deal with is the observable and the verifiable.

Now they will admit that there is much about the world that they don't understand, but that isn't an admission of *inability to explain*. Not knowing all the facts yet, and not being *able* to understand the facts, are two entirely different things. They will admit that they don't understand all the processes involved in the universe and they don't know how it all started and formed into what we see now; but they would never admit to the fact that there is no answer from a human point of view. They feel certain that if one of them had been present when the solar system began, he would have been quite able to observe, take notes, collect samples, and write up an adequate description of what happened that satisfies man's curiosity. The fact that they don't know what happened isn't due to an inability to understand, but simply because nobody saw it happen – an unfortunate accident of fate, that's all.

They despise the idea of introducing God into the picture. The aim of their research is to uncover how matter and energy shaped itself into the present universe; they feel sure that matter and energy can shape itself into galaxies and planets and grass and scientists – there is no need to introduce God into the picture in order to explain all this, they say, because it is simply a matter of the fortuitous arrangement of the elements over time and space. And since that's true – since existence is at our eye level, so to speak, so that we can easily see and understand the whole process if given enough time and scientific experience – then everything is, by definition, explainable.

Please understand what I mean by the word "explainable." It's not that we can say something about it, whatever that might be. If we can explain something then we can describe all of its parts, and the relationships between the parts, and exactly how it works, and especially how it first came to exist. Scientists say that they can't explain life yet, for example, because they don't know exactly what happens inside a living organism that we describe with the word "life". For that reason they don't know how to duplicate it in their test tubes. If they ever did figure out life to the extent that they could duplicate it, then they could say that they have "explained" it satisfactorily. Until that time it remains an unexplainable phenomenon; we can easily talk about it and describe many things about it, but we can't do it ourselves because we don't know its hidden secrets.

Christians giving up ground

Christians should never admit the unbeliever's premise. Scientists wrongly assume that everything is explainable, and it's a serious mistake for us to let them hold that notion. The trouble is that we have, in fact, given them the freedom to believe that and therefore we've given them what they need to defeat us. We are our own worst enemy.

Over the last two hundred years science has made great strides in many disciplines. Man has come to understand amazing things about the world – he not only understands it but he knows how to manipulate it to serve his purposes. It's probably been the greatest success story of our time, this accelerated progress of science. But the Church has been dazzled along the way too, and as science explained more and more of our world the Church found herself increasingly unable to challenge any of its statements. After all, how can you argue with something that is so obvious and reasonable?

So the Church had no option but to play along with the game. To save face, she devised a scheme where both parties could be happy: science is the expert in the physical realm, and the Church is the expert in the spiritual realm. The Bible, she said, is not a textbook for science – or for mathematics or political science or economics or any other branch of human learning. It is a textbook on specifically spiritual matters. In fact, for the last two hundred years the game has gone something like this: man discovers a new area of study, he creates a professional field for it complete with professors, experts, theories, schools, etc., and the Church graciously backs out to give the new field room to grow on its own. The Church refuses to dictate to these experts what the moral limits are, what the methods of conducting their study should be, and the goals that they should be working for.

In all this the Church keeps hoping that its "spiritual" contribution will somehow bless and corral what the world is doing, but it's a false hope. We've painted ourselves into a corner and nobody is taking us seriously any more. By failing to challenge the false premise of the unbelievers we've actually cut ourselves off from the world, and they are out there running rampant with no controls and no idea of the judgment that is gathering around their heads. We talk about our "spiritual" domain and they don't pay any attention to us, because such things don't have anything to do with the "real" world.

It was a foolish philosophical blunder. Regarding this matter of Creation, for instance, it amounted to handing the unbeliever a gun with which he can kill us. We are saying to him that yes, it is true that science can better explain the process of how the world came to be, and the Bible wasn't meant to be a science textbook. The unbeliever, therefore, immediately takes that gun and aims it at our heads with the statement "Well, then, it can be explained without having to bring God into it!" If science *can* understand and explain how the world came to be, then the purpose of the Bible's story of Creation is no more than to give us a warm comfortable feeling that somehow (not scientifically at any rate!) God was overseeing the process. The final outcome is that science doesn't need God to explain the world and we agree!

It's time that we took stock of the situation and changed tactics. It may be too late, it may be that the gun is smoking and we are dying, but we still need to come to our senses and realize what we've done wrong. We cannot allow the unbeliever's premise any more. Science is wrong: at the root of the whole world – in other words, in Creation – is something that they cannot explain. The Church alone holds the key to understanding Creation.

Perhaps in no other area is the Church so guilty of handing the victory to the enemy as in our own attempts at scientifically explaining the Bible away. There is certainly a place for science in the work of the Church; we alone can appreciate the perfection and balance and purpose and beauty that the Almighty built into the whole world. A scientist tries to uncover every ingredient of what he is studying, and we certainly have the advantage over everyone else since we know the Creator personally. But it is a fundamental error to start with science when we want to learn about Creation; it can give us no guidelines for how to start. Too many Christians don't understand that. In order to answer the question, "How did the universe come to be what it is?", we should never start by saying "Just look at the design, the obvious purpose, the wisdom behind it all". That answer isn't good enough; unbelievers are ignoring it because, even though the evidence looks pretty convincing, they know we haven't proved the existence of God yet, let alone whether or not he was responsible for Creation.

The Lord expects us to start with *revelation*, not science, if we want to understand any of his works. He has things to tell us *before* we start our scientific studies that will guide us in arriving at the correct conclusions. Before man can understand anything, God must reveal Truth to him. This is especially true in matters where God's honor is at stake, as it is in this matter of who created the universe! We have to come to him and learn the fundamentals of truth before we can go to the world and detect his hand in it. We have to believe that the world is not the source of ultimate truth about God; and we also have to believe that whatever truth that the world may contain, we have severe limitations (because of our sin and ignorance) that prevent our digging it out. Only by hearing God's Truth will we know what is actually going on.

The simplest saint should be able to understand the truth about Creation. It is not necessary to know a lot about science in order to know the truth; if it were, then most of us would have to leave the discussion up to the experts to handle. But Creation isn't a matter for experts, either Christian or non-Christian; it is an area about which anybody who has faith can be informed, and anybody who believes the Scripture can speak with authority.

What we need right now, in other words, is not more scientific proofs that God created the world, but the testimony of Scripture. We need the revelation of God, the proclamation of what he has done, because in it he will tell us what he did and how he did it and what we should do with it. Let him speak first! Then we will know how to handle our studies in a way that will properly honor the Creator.

Scriptural foundation

A primary passage in this regard is Hebrews 11, which reads like this:

By faith we understand that the universe was formed at God's command, so that what is seen was not made out of what was visible. (Hebrews 11:3)

This verse, which talks about Creation, teaches us at least three things about what God did in the beginning:

- **Whatever actually happened, only faith will enable us to understand it.** Science cannot. Reason cannot. Logic and observation cannot. You may not realize the limitations that this verse puts on man when it comes to the subject of Creation; what he sees with his eyes, what he touches with his hands, what he hears and smells, what he monitors on any instruments that he can devise, are *unable* to help him explain how the world came to be.

Faith, as you will find when you study the Bible, is the ability to see the spiritual realities of God's world. The process of faith runs like this: *first*, God tells man what he did or will do; he may offer an explanation and he may not, but in any case the Word of God illuminates the situation with light from another world. *Second*, man sees that it is not of this world – this thing that God shows us is obviously spiritual. This step is crucial for the process of faith because it convinces us that we're dealing with a bigger world than our minds can conceive or understand. *Third*, man depends on what God told him – this is *truth*. We understand that there is a spiritual foundation underneath our physical world that holds us up, guides us in spiritual channels, and judges us with penetrating wisdom. For a case study of what the Bible specifically defines as true faith, study Romans 4 and the "father of our faith", Abraham.

Creation is just as much a matter of faith as any other aspect of the works of God. In this case it is a past event, but it is nevertheless an event that is clearly impossible in man's eyes. How could the world be made in six days? How could mountains and grass and oceans obey God? How can the birds actually be "blessed"? But the impossibility of the whole thing is just what faith is looking for here! If we had an entirely reasonable explanation then the unbelievers would be right – God isn't necessary. But that's not how the story reads! It describes the impossible, what only God could do, something that is beyond our ability to explain.

The story demands our faith, not our understanding. Don't misunderstand me; I'm not saying that Christians have to set aside their minds in order to please God. But in the case of Creation we will never understand how he made the universe, and we aren't expected to be able to explain it scientifically, because he is a God who does the impossible. He speaks and the world exists; he speaks and the creatures are blessed. *We need the God who made the world in this way.* We don't need a passive, weak, stupid god who lets the world work out its own destiny; we don't need an apathetic god who doesn't care if things work out or not. We need nothing less than a God who can make the world in 6 days! We want this God of magnificent power, of inconceivable wisdom, of driving authority, of relentless purpose to be our God as well. Let's not find little ways to explain him out of the picture – let's believe that everything literally depends on him in every way!

Hear what the Bible is saying to us. It is calling science's bluff, so to speak; it is challenging its basic premise. Not everything is explainable; this story says that Creation itself, which is at the root of all existence, and from which all things have come, is a massive, unexplainable event. Science cannot tell us how the world came to be because it doesn't use faith to grasp hold of the subject. It uses sensors and detectors and computers and microscopes and telescopes, without realizing that it has yet to pick up the one tool that will enable it to see what actually happened.

Faith serves a critical function for the Christian: it brings him in touch with a God who can make good on all the promises in the Scriptures. Man has tried for millennia to improve life, to get along with each other, to eradicate suffering and death, to improve everyone's lot in life – and failed miserably over and over again. God, however, declared that he can do it – he holds out that hope to whoever will believe. Without faith, however, nobody will be convinced that God can really do what man has found impossible; until, of course, he is actually brought before the throne of the Almighty and he sees this God. Through faith a person finally believes that God is quite capable of doing anything he wants to do!

Now this person who has seen God can turn around and believe that all this universe came from God's hand. He knows that the world is built on miracles, on an act of God that man can't explain and certainly can't duplicate himself. Instead of starting out on the wrong foot he starts out his science with reverence, with fear, with the knowledge that nothing exists without the direct involvement of the Lord.

We can put it another way. Suppose that a team of scientists were present at the Creation, with all the instruments and sampling methods that they could wish for. The end result of their observation would be simply this: they would come away from the event without any data. They would be at a complete loss to describe what they saw. The reason for this is because *one can't explain the miraculous*. How could a scientist have explained Jesus walking on water? How could an expert in fluid dynamics explained Elijah's miracle of making the axe head float in water? How can a chemist explain water turning into wine? The answer is obvious: there is no explanation. That's why scientists call these stories myths – they claim that such things couldn't possibly have happened. In the same way, there is no scientific explanation for Creation. What happened there is a matter for faith to get hold of, not scientific instruments. We first have to see the God who created the world before we will see the amazing nature of his work.

This means, then, that Genesis 1 is a lot more accurate than even we Christians have been willing to admit. Science has nothing on us here. It may look as if the events in the history of the universe were self-determined and perfectly in line with the laws of physics, all the way back to when the first atoms came together to form the galaxies and stars and planets, but in fact they were not. It all started out with a miraculous event that had no resemblance with existence as we know it now.

- **The process of Creation was God's command.** This verse in Hebrews also tells us plainly that the universe didn't come about from physical or atomic or geologic or evolutionary processes working to produce the world that we now have. It happened by an entirely different process – the commands of God.

Science doesn't have a category for this type of thing. Traditionally it has always said in response to our doctrine, "OK, at the most it simply means that God used normal processes like evolution or geology to make the world." "God commanded" gets translated into "God used normal, explainable procedures to do what he wanted." But that is wrong on at least two counts: **first**, he used impossible miracles elsewhere in the Bible to do his will – it seems that we can't always limit him to working through normal procedures. **Second**, it's like talking out of both sides of one's mouth; we say on the one hand that he "commanded" things to happen, and then we say that these things happened through normal, universal processes. Which is it going to be?

The darling of science is the principle of cause and effect. When a scientist sees something happen – an event in time and space – he always assumes that there was a cause and that it is detectable and measurable. For instance, in 1846 Leverrier discovered the planet Neptune by noticing that Uranus wasn't where it should have been according to predictions – presumably another planet was tugging at Uranus with its own gravity and altering its position. Through mathematics Leverrier predicted where the new planet would be in the sky and how big it was, and the astronomers turned their telescopes to that spot – there was the new planet, which they named Neptune. It was a classic case of cause and effect.

That's all right for normal events, but the principle of cause and effect falls useless to the ground when we are dealing with extraordinary events. (For that matter everything is extraordinary, when you think about it; even the law of cause and effect is a specially designed principle that nicely orders our world for us. It's just that the present extraordinary system that we live in is different from the extraordinary time of Creation.) In the case of Creation, the cause of living things was not an evolutionary process of simple organisms adapting and changing into complex organisms; the text says:

And God said, "Let the water teem with living creatures, and let birds fly above the earth across the expanse of the sky." (Genesis 1:20)

And God said, "Let the land produce living creatures according to their kinds: livestock, creatures that move along the ground, and wild animals, each according to its kind." (Genesis 1:24)

Then God said, "Let us make man in our image, in our likeness." (Genesis 1:26)

The cause, in other words, for these living creatures was the *command of God*. Life came from God's order, not from chance or evolution. How did that happen? Nobody knows! A scientist would have seen trees springing up out of the earth, and animals bubbling up from out of the ground, and man coming together from the dust of the earth. And if he had ears to hear, he would have heard a command precede each event. None of it would have made sense to him, but there it was anyway.

It's interesting how often the Bible talks about creation responding in obedience to God's commands. Who obeyed God's order that animals be formed from the ground? The ground and the animals obeyed! Does this make sense to us? Of course not; but we are out of our depth here – this is material that can only be understood by God. When he commands, *everything* listens; it doesn't matter if something is inanimate or animate, unintelligent or intelligent. God's command has a creative power that enables matter and energy to do what it can't do on its own; it is the only thing that explains satisfactorily why the world is the way it is.

The reason why creation jumps in obedience is because of who God is. He is the Master, the Lord, the original "despot" (which is the Greek word in 2 Peter 2:1) who expects nothing less than strict and immediate obedience to whatever he says. This is the "cause" of creation, the reason why everything turned out like it did. There was nothing inherent in anything that dictated its form or function; there was no blueprint in its genes or atomic structure that determined what it would look like. All that is true now, of course, because creation continues being what it is – it produces more "after its own kind" which is the blueprint principle. But the original plan, the first time when things fell into their places, was the scene at Creation when God made everything by command, out of nothing.

Why are stones hard? The scientist tells us that it is due to the nature of the atoms and molecules that make up the stone. But I ask, why are the atoms the way they are, and why are they arranged in such a way as to make this stone? At some point the scientist has to throw up his hands and plead ignorance, if he doesn't actually say that it isn't important. But I answer that it is desperately important; what would we do if stones weren't like what they are? The only satisfactory answer to the problem, the only answer that will tell us the why and the how of everything in life (including all the categories of normal life like "purpose" and "suitability" that scientists don't like to talk about but they depend on every day) is that God commanded everything to be the way it is. The stone is simply obeying the creative Word that was issued at the beginning of time. It is what it is because God wanted it to be the way it is. This is a universe of obedience, not impersonal random motions of matter. We have to take even the law of cause and effect with a grain of salt; it *looks* as if an event occurred because of what prompted it, what came before it, but really both events and things are simply obeying the blueprint that God wrote into their makeup at Creation.

- **The stuff of creation was not creation itself.** Hebrews 11:3 tells us that matter and energy – along with the "laws" that govern both – came out of *nothing*. [7] One minute the universe didn't exist in any form whatsoever; the next minute, a world was there.

This runs directly contrary to another of science's favorite maxims: "Matter and energy can neither be created nor destroyed." One can turn into the other, but they are fundamentally eternal. A scientist thinks that it is absurd to believe that matter came from nothing; if he would believe that, he argues, then there's no telling when and where and how matter might show up again. He can't operate in a world that isn't completely predictable, completely understandable and easily manipulated.

But there's the sticking point. Chaos isn't the only alternative to the dilemma. If one believes that God made the universe and he did it through unconventional means, then the universe hangs on God's bare will. We are what we are simply because God decided to make us like this. This means that the future of the universe hangs on his will, too; we can't predict what will happen to the world by studying its present behavior. Science can't help us understand the beginning or the end of existence, because it doesn't have the equipment to deal with the purposes

---

[7] The verse actually says this: "so as what is seen did not come into being from things that are seen." This simply says, on the surface, that the world wasn't made from itself. In other words, it refutes the idea that matter is eternal; it teaches us that matter and energy, the building blocks of the material universe, had a definite beginning before which they did not exist.

and plans of God. This is solely the department of the Church.

Scripture tells us that yes, things do come out from nowhere – at God's command. Nothing is chaotic, everything is dependable, the universe is stable – because God is responsible for everything. He will make sure that the rocks stay rocks, and the laws of thermodynamics continue to hold true, and "season follows season", and the oceans will stay in their defined boundaries. But there's nothing inherent in the nature of matter that makes it continue to exist, or to move in particular ways. One day we will see how "eternal" matter is when God destroys (to the scientist, an impossible notion) the "elements" and remakes everything. (2 Peter 3:10) Then we will see that Christ does indeed "hold all things together", (Colossians 1:17) "sustaining all things by his powerful Word." (Hebrews 1:3) Without him the universe would snap back into non-existence.

The way things work now, however, is by the principle "according to its kind." Science looks at our present situation and falsely reasons backward, thinking that the processes that run our world have always held true – even at the beginning. Well, in certain ways it is true that "matter and energy can neither be created nor destroyed;" we see that and depend on it and use it to guide our discoveries. In another way, however, that very law depends on God's will and it can easily be superseded when he so chooses. See the miracles of the Bible for proof of this point. In the meantime, however, we can build our lives around the scheme of things that God has set up temporarily in our world. But it didn't start out that way, and it isn't going to end up that way. It is only here, in between cataclysmic events, that science has phenomena to observe; it needs to step aside and let the

Bible tell us of how things were in the beginning and how things will be at the end of time, when the normal laws of nature are set aside.

Moses' account the best explanation

Now, is it really true that the Bible has nothing scientific to say about Creation? Is it true that science can better explain what happened at the beginning? Many people think that it is, that Genesis 1 is simply "myth" or symbolic language that gives us the correct religious feeling about God and his activities but not a scientifically accurate picture of Creation – let science teach us that, they say.

But if, on the contrary, the above points are true, the Bible has a lot to say about Creation. In fact, it insists on having the dominant word on the matter – the only valid explanation of what happened. The Hebrews 11 passage alerts us to the fact that science is woefully deficient when it comes to being able to explain how the world came to be. Science can *never* tell us what really happened. It was a work of God, beyond man's ability to understand and explain, and to even try to explain it scientifically is to attempt either to see things from God's point of view (which a creature can't do, by definition) or to boil it all down to natural and understandable events that don't require a God. Either way, looking to science to explain Creation is a sell-out, treason in the ranks, a taking away of God's glory.

No, the picture is actually quite plain in the Bible. Given the correct principles to start with (which we established from Hebrews 11:3), one has to conclude that the account that Moses gave us in Genesis 1 is really the best possible explanation of what really happened. *It can't be said more correctly than the way he said it.* As a matter of fact, if someone had actually been there when it happened, he would have explained what he saw just as we have it recorded here in Genesis 1. There is no other way to say it without being misleading and entirely wrong. Nobody can make an improvement on the details. It is true that science can explain much (not all, however!) of the world in its present state, but it has nothing to say about Creation.

Fight the temptation

However, it is not an easy thing to live in this sophisticated world of ours. Scientists won't quit, and atheists work hard at chipping away at the faith. It seems that every day more discoveries crop up that point away from the Bible's account of Creation, that more and more evidence points to an ultimate explanation of the universe. There are scientists working right now on that question – how did the universe get the way it is? Physicists and astronomers and geologists and specialists from many fields are pushing back the limits of human understanding with the hope that someday a "unified theory" will take shape, a theory that any layman can understand, which will explain the deepest mysteries of existence.

What does a Christian do in a time like this? We have to be careful here: there's a difference between living by faith and living by what is often called "blind faith". Living by faith is taking seriously what the Bible teaches us, even (or especially!) when man contradicts it; living by "blind faith" usually refers to closing one's eyes to the discoveries of science for no good reason. The pursuit of science is good – if one fears God at the same time. A man can certainly discover and explain how many things in the world operate, and he can take advantage of that knowledge to improve his level of living. That's good science. But when someone turns his back on what the Bible expressly teaches, simply because he refuses to believe in God, and intentionally looks for an explanation that cuts God out of what is rightfully his place, that's when science isn't doing its job.

Still, it isn't so easy to turn away from the convincing arguments of the experts. They often paint the picture in false colors: they tell us that they are discovering that one doesn't need to use God to explain things, and our Christian view is terribly inaccurate – it doesn't coincide with the facts that they are finding. But just hang in there, Christian; you will discover several things about unbelieving scientists if you wait them out. **First**, their theories are always changing. The history of science is replete with examples of arrogant men predicting the downfall of religion and the amazing ability of their new theories to explain reality. In a few years their theories are gone from everywhere but the schools (schools seem to hang on to outmoded theories for a long time!) and a new set of theories with new heroes have stepped onto the stage that completely repudiates the old set of theories. It's an interesting show to watch. Isn't it significant that our body of knowledge hasn't changed a bit over 4000 years?

Second, their false arrogance inevitably covers over faulty data or bad research. They usually make a fatal mistake in their eagerness to cut the feet out from under the Christians: they don't explain *everything*, contrary to their arrogant claims, and we often find that they made mistakes that gave rise to the results they got. For example, there has been a massive push going on lately to discover life on planets in other stellar systems besides our own. The idea is that if they can discover life there, it would go a long way to disproving the Christian doctrine that life is unique on earth. They would wave it in front of our faces and say, "See here? It doesn't take a God to create life! It happens wherever the physical circumstances are conducive to its existence." But their logic is faulty; in their rush to embarrass us they stumbled over some basic principles of good science. One error they are committing is a logical fallacy called "hasty generalization"; they assume that, since life happened here, it could happen elsewhere too. But one occurrence doesn't prove that there would be more! The scientific method is to observe at least several occurrences before one draws conclusions about it. And it is especially important to not jump to conclusions about the universality of life in light of the fact that life occurs here on earth *against impossible odds* – study astronomy some time and you will see what I mean. Life occurred here *in spite of* the way the universe is, not because of it. Again, this is an example of God doing the impossible. My point is this: you will find that scientists often don't do good work when they are busy undermining the truth of the Bible.

In the meantime, how should we Christians handle this matter of Creation? Since we believe that it was a miraculous act of God, best described by Genesis 1, what effect is that belief going to have on how we live and work? In the *first* place, it should give us confidence in the work of God and a deeper understanding of how he does things. We needn't be scared off any more by the arguments of the unbelievers. They simply don't know what they are talking about. They failed to get the first principles down, the foundation stones that one needs to understand the works of God. We have those foundation stones since we have gone to God's revelation about what happened at Creation. Although the unbelieving scientists will find useful ways of getting profit from our world, and we can benefit from their work, they don't understand the things about Creation that man needs to know in order to find joy and peace; whatever slanders they come up with against our Creator and Redeemer we can safely dismiss as spiritual ignorance.

Second, we ourselves need to study at the feet of the Master. We can do science too; we also have minds that are capable of analyzing the world and using scientific results. But we have to get all the firsts principles down before we go running off to study God's works. Not only do we have to know that God created the world, we have to learn why he created it, and what he has in mind for everything. Righteousness, for example, is built into all his works and we mustn't be like little children who are ignorant of righteousness. (Hebrews 5:11-14) We have already seen that the world exists in obedience to God's commands – so we need to study his commands and what a life of obedience is like. We need to know this King who rules his subjects – animal and rock and man alike – so that we will work with him instead of against him. We have also got to learn our own place in the scheme of things; remember that God gave us a duty at the Creation to rule over this world in his Name, in his image – do we understand what it means to rule over subjects (which entails protecting them and helping them reach fulfillment and building everything together into a harmonious and glorious whole), and are we willing and ready to obey that command? You see, in order to do science you must first know a good deal about God.

Third, when you do your science you must keep in mind what you learned from the revelation of God. Never forget the lessons that you learned in the King's court. Be careful to obey his will, to steer your research into avenues that will bring glory to him and help to others. Remember, for instance, that this world was designed to obey its Creator, each part in its own way, and the result is the will of God on earth. As a scientist you are obligated to find out what his will is and contribute with your own obedience – as a regent of the King – to "do all things for the glory of God."

Why Creation is a matter of faith

148

Lot:
A Vindication
of a
Righteous Man

Introduction

There are some stories in the Bible that, at first glance, would seem obvious as far as their meaning. But when one studies it more, and digs around for other passages that may enlighten it further, it appears that what used to be obvious isn't obvious any more. We just may be guilty of applying our own preconceived notions to the text and making it say what it doesn't say at all. We especially have reason to suspect this is true when another passage of Scripture makes a point-blank statement about the first passage, and when the second passage's interpretation of the first directly contradicts our interpretation.

The story of Lot is a good example of this. I believe that too many Bible students have looked at the superficial aspects of the story and come away with a false interpretation of it; and what makes me feel this way is that the passage of 2 Peter 2:6-9 directly contradicts *their* interpretation of the story of Lot. All the signs point to something being wrong here.

What we want to do in this study, therefore, is examine the story of Lot in light of the Peter passage and see if we arrive at different conclusions than if we didn't have Peter's account. We will find, I believe, that it would be safer to pick on someone else in the Bible before calling Lot an unrighteous man, a sinner who didn't care about the sin of the Sodomites, who suffered the consequences of his sin – all of which students tend to find in this story. In fact, we have more hard proof of the sins of other Bible characters than we have for Lot!

If this premise is true – if Lot really is righteous and the usual charges against him are false – then why do people pick on him so much? I think that it's a classic case of going strictly by appearances instead of probing through the veil with God-given faith. If we start with only what we see, then our results will be what our common sense and reason tell us is true; if we start with revelation (which is God showing us what we would never have known otherwise) then we will get what the Scripture tells us is true – which is usually the opposite of what our reason would have found. Faith is the key to interpreting the Bible correctly, and "faith comes from hearing the message, and the message is heard through the Word of Christ." (Romans 10:17)

The reason we have to explore this issue about Lot and clear up the confusion is because of what I believe the story is about: God rescuing the righteous. Another word for "rescue" is "deliverance" – which is what the entire ministry of Christ is about. What we need is more encouragement to believe and hold fast to the Savior who will rescue us from sin and death. The Scripture is given to us to encourage us in this; the way it does it is to show us the Savior in action, and others getting saved. "Therefore, since we are surrounded by such a great cloud of witnesses, let us throw off everything that hinders and the sin that so easily entangles and let us run with perseverance the race marked out for us." (Hebrews 12:1) The witnesses that it speaks of are those who have found the Lord to be a capable and faithful deliverer; Lot also found him to be the same thing in his situation. And we can't afford to ignore this story of deliverance, but rather we must pay attention to it and learn from it. "How shall we escape if we ignore such a great salvation?" (Hebrews 2:3) Lot escaped from disaster, and we need to study his story so that we will also escape from the wrath to come.

Problems with Lot

People have had more problems with Lot than perhaps any other character in the Bible. It's always "open season" on Lot when students study the Genesis account of his life; he seems to do nothing right in their opinion. If the rest of Scripture was silent about him, we might just accept the fact that he was a failure and learn from his mistakes.

But the Bible isn't silent about Lot. It makes a paradoxical statement about him that forces us either to disagree or go back to Genesis looking for something that we must have missed. If we claim to believe what the Bible teaches, and if we want to be honest Bible students and find out exactly what it says apart from our own opinions, then we must find a solution to this problem about Lot. We can't afford to let this paradox go unsolved.

First let's assemble all the problem areas in the story of Lot and see what we are up against.

What do people accuse him of?

According to most modern students, Lot committed just about every sin in the book. They claim that if Lot was really a child of God, it was only by the skin of his teeth – he certainly doesn't deserve God's mercy in light of the way he lived.

Let's list some of the sins that Lot was supposed to have committed:

- **Turning away from Canaan and the promise of God** – The Lord gave his promises and covenant to Abraham; by being with Abraham, Lot was assured of the blessings of God. But he turned away from the covenant, and away from living with other believers, and therefore couldn't expect any of the things that Abraham enjoyed.

- **Lusting after this world's goodness** – He saw the well-watered plains of the Jordan, and he turned and looked at the rugged mountains of Palestine, and then made up his mind: comfort, ease and prosperity, instead of wandering, opposition and hardship.

153

- **Making his home among the wicked** – It says that "the men of Sodom were wicked and were sinning greatly against the Lord." (Genesis 13:13) Yet Lot chose that place to live! How could he leave the company of the righteous and go to live with some of the most wicked people on earth?

- **Making his business his god** – He obviously had an eye to expanding his business and increasing his wealth; he could do that most easily in an urban setting where there was plenty of opportunity for buying and selling and trading. He couldn't expect such great profits by wandering like Abraham!

- **Buying into the world's system by getting on the city council at Sodom** – The text says that "Lot was sitting in the gateway of the city." (Genesis 19:1) In those days, the gate was where the leading elders of the city sat to discuss current events and decide the laws to govern the people. By being among them, we see that Lot was one of the trusted leaders of the people – he surely must have compromised himself to get to such a position of trust with wicked men!

- **Failing to train his children in the fear of the Lord** – By the way the story of Lot ends, we can see easily enough that Lot's children were just as reprobate as the Sodomites were. Obviously Lot failed in his duties as a father – perhaps his business was more important to him?

- **Failing to teach his wife about God and expecting godly submission from her** – Again, the story bears out the point that Lot's wife didn't have the things of God in mind; she loved her city, and thought that the fear of the

154

Lord was a small matter when she saw her beloved possessions destroyed. Lot obviously didn't teach his family the truth about God.

- **Not finding godly sons-in-law for his daughters** – They refused to listen to his plea to leave the city; if they were believers in God, and feared his Word, they would have followed the angels out of Sodom. Didn't Lot care what kind of young men would marry his daughters? Shouldn't he have discerned their unbelief earlier and forbade his daughters to be engaged to them?

- **Offering his daughters for illicit sex** – Probably the most shocking part of the story. In order to "protect" the angels from the crowd of reprobates, he offers his daughters to them "to do what you like with them." (Genesis 19.8) Every loving and responsible parent shudders at the thought while reading that.

- **Loving Sodom too much to leave** – Even when the angels pled with Lot to leave Sodom, he found excuses not to go. They had to drag him out!

- **Arguing with the Lord** – Instead of simply accepting the Lord's command to go to the mountains, Lot argued with God – as if he knew better what was good for him! And he argued for what he wanted, his own desires, in the face of God's expressed will. Is this the heart of a child of God?

- **Getting drunk** – An obvious failure, where he drowns his misery in drink – which is all too common among those who rebel against God's commands and end up paying the penalty for their sin.

- **Fathering his own grandchildren** – As if trying to outdo their father in unthinkable family relations, his daughters plot how to further their own family lines and make Lot guilty of incest. Now, for the rest of his life he would have to live daily with these two reminders of his spiritual failures.

If only half of these things were true about Lot, we could hardly consider him a righteous man. We could justifiably say that the Lord gave Lot his due by bringing him into misery in the end.

That raises another perspective on the story of Lot. It's obvious, isn't it, that Lot consistently made bad decisions in life that ruined his end? He decided to part company with Abraham and therefore Abraham's God, he decided to live with the wicked, he decided that his business was more important than fellowship with the saints, he decided it would be good for his business to be involved in the local government, he decided that it would be better to sacrifice his family for the good of the whole, he decided that living in towns was better than living in the mountains. Where did all these bad decisions get him in the end? A broken man, penniless, no business or money left, wife and sons-in-law dead, nowhere to lived and daughters committing incest! This shows without doubt that when a man decides his own way of living, he is going to find God twisting his path, making his way "a hedge of thorns", and all will end in disaster.

You may wonder how anybody could think well of Lot, after reading about all these sins of his! But my main point is that *all this is a slander against a righteous man*. Lot doesn't deserve the bad reputation that he has gotten from the modern Church. In fact, once we find out the truth about the man, we Christians should hope that we might be as faithful and devoted a believer as Lot was!

There are many reasons why people think these things against Lot, which we will look at in a minute. But in light of what the final conclusion of the Bible is when it discusses Lot, we ought to be very careful what we say against him. What we think he did wrong may very well be *our* mistake!

I'm sure that when Christians step into Heaven and see Lot standing there, they are going to point their fingers at him and say, "What are *you* doing here?" We can't imagine that God would be at all happy with the way Lot lived in this world. But I believe that Lot will answer us with this: "The same reason *you* are here!" Our salvation depends solely on God's grace, and his grace works through our faith in him. Lot had no less faith in God than we have; in fact, according to the testimony of Scripture about him, he probably felt less at ease in the world he lived in than we do in ours.

Bad interpretations

It seems that when people read the story of Lot, they break every rule in the book trying to interpret what the Scripture says about him. Rules of interpretation are simply effective ways of getting at the truth of a passage. If you want to want to learn what a particular passage is teaching, then use these helpful methods to dig out the correct interpretation. Break these rules, however, and you are going to end up with falsehood instead of truth – you will miss what God wants you to learn from it.

For example, the most common rule that students break while working with the story of Lot is this: *don't read things in between the lines*. Too many times we come to a passage ready to read something that isn't there; we often find, when talking to others about it, that we *thought* that the passage says such and such when it really doesn't say any such thing. We *want* it to say something, it's obvious to us that it *means* that, so we claim that it *does* teach that.

People say that Lot decided to leave Abraham and go his own way. But he didn't decide anything of the sort! A careful reading will show you that *Abraham* decided to send Lot away. If anything, Abraham is at fault for the things that happened to Lot.

People say that Lot got drunk. But the text doesn't say that at all. He drank wine – that's all it says. The Bible says that Noah got *drunk*, that Nabal got *drunk*, that Uriah the Hittite got *drunk*, but it doesn't say that Lot got drunk. Yet sermons have focused on Lot the miserable old man drowning his misery with wine, something the Scripture doesn't teach at all.

People say that Lot knowingly went to live among the wicked men of Sodom. But the Scripture doesn't say at all whether Lot *knew* they were wicked. As we will see below, chances are good that he didn't know the extent of their sin and was simply settling down among people like you and I know – people who turn out, just like our neighbors, to be worse than we originally thought.

People say that Lot was motivated by his greed; that's why he left Abraham and the land of the Covenant. But the text doesn't say he was a greedy man, nor does it say that he put business ahead of spiritual communion with the faithful. In fact, it says that he moved to a community *for the same reason* that we ourselves make career and residence changes! If we blame him for that, we must also blame ourselves.

We could go on, but hopefully you see my point. We ought to be careful and read exactly what it says, not what we are hoping it says in order to support our own opinions.

Another rule of interpretation that students aren't careful to follow is that *Scripture interprets Scripture*. This means that the Bible has the right to say, before anybody else speaks, what the meaning of a passage is. If it takes advantage of that right and tells us how to read a story, then we must submit to its view and change ours if necessary. In fact, when the Bible tells us what to believe about a story, it's usually because we would never have got that meaning out of it ourselves.

The Bible does make use of its privilege in this case: 2 Peter 2:6-8. And its interpretation of the story of Lot is startlingly different than the one we would have come up with without divine help. We will see later how important this passage is when we try to understand Lot; but for now we must realize what the Bible is doing: it's setting the record straight, giving us the truth about Lot.

Remember that the Scriptures are "God-breathed" – the Word of God, not of man, and absolutely correct in all that it teaches. This is the Truth; all other views are only true if they conform to this standard. So when one passage makes a statement about some other passage, what it says is the only right way of interpreting the second passage. This is a cardinal rule to keep in mind when doing Bible study. "The Bible is its own best interpreter," goes the old saying.

One other rule of interpretation that students tend to ignore with the story of Lot is *comparing Scripture with Scripture*. One must use the same meanings of words, and the same spiritual principles, that are fully developed in the rest of the Bible. For instance, did Lot come to a miserable end? Isn't that proof that the Lord was simply paying him out for the bad decisions he made in life? Not so! There are other examples in Scripture of people who came to miserable ends and it was no fault of their own. Lazarus, for example, who lived and died miserably, yet was counted a righteous man for all that. (Luke 16:20-22) Other examples are the saints listed in Hebrews 11, who "were all commended for their faith, yet none of them received what had been promised." (Hebrews 11:39)

Jesus himself challenged the notion that people *always* experience physical disasters because of spiritual problems. (Luke 13:1-5) He told his disciples that a man who was born blind wasn't therefore proved to be a sinner; his blindness, instead, was for the purpose of glorifying God. (John 9:1-5) And in Ecclesiastes we read about "righteous men who get what the wicked deserve, and wicked men who get what the righteous deserve" (Ecclesiastes 8:14) – a sobering principle in a world lacking meaning.

But probably the crowning injustice that people commit against Lot concerns his so-called "sin" of settling in Sodom. It usually goes like this: Lot sinned against God, against the light of truth that he had while living with Abraham, by shutting his eyes to the wickedness of that city and putting business goals ahead of the moral problems that he was bound to be exposed to by living there. At the very least, when he learned the full extent of the Sodomites' wickedness, he should have gotten himself and his family out of there. Then in the same breath, these people claim that we too live in a modern-day Sodom and we have to "separate" ourselves from the surrounding wickedness. So, stay close to the Lord, and don't live as our neighbors do.

This is called spiritualizing a text because it's convenient to do so. If the answer for Lot was to *get out* of Sodom, and we live in a Sodom too, then the answer for us too is to *leave the country we are in!* Either the answer is spiritual in both cases, or the answer is physical in both cases; but we can't have it both ways and be fair to the text – or to Lot. If we can live in a wicked society and stay separate from it, then so could Lot. And if Peter is right about Lot's character, he probably did as well as, or even better than, we do in our situations. As we will see later, Peter didn't spiritualize the text, so we don't have the liberty to do that either.

Requires faith

Sometimes we get too sure of ourselves when studying the Bible. We think that this book is easy to understand, that it's like any other book and can be understood with just a little effort on our part. We forget that this is mystery, a revelation of God and his ways, something that we wouldn't otherwise know if God hadn't bent down to our level and made it plain to our darkened minds.

Don't be too sure of yourself when reading the story of Lot. You may have many neat categories of right and wrong that you can fit the details into, but you may be surprised at what God is doing in the story – and in your heart as you read. This book requires faith to get the point, not persistence or cunning or intelligence.

Faith is being able to see the things of God in spite of what the world puts up in the way. As Hebrews 11:1 puts it, faith is being "certain of what we do not see." It's not just *being* certain that makes true faith; it's *what we are certain about* that makes us the faithful. Many people are sure of what *they* believe; but not many people are sure about what God *says*.

One area (we could discuss many here!) where we must approach something with faith is this matter of what the Bible teaches. You would think that it's simply a matter of believing what it says and that is that! But it's much more difficult than that. Many things stand in the way of believing the Bible: for example, tradition often teaches things contrary to what the Bible teaches, and tradition demands our loyalty. "This is what people have always believed and I must believe it also!" Another problem area is common sense: one meaning or interpretation makes more sense than another, and it would be foolish for me to believe something that doesn't apparently fit in with the rest of my opinions (or systems of truth, as we proudly call them.)

The story of Lot suffers from both these approaches. To simply believe what Peter says about Lot, without discrimination, without even noticing that something may be wrong in his life, doesn't square with common sense or traditional teaching. So we don't believe what Peter says about him. We won't baldly admit such a thing – we will say, instead, that Lot was righteous but only in a judicial sense of being forgiven, not in a practical sense – but the sum of it is that we don't have the faith to believe what Scripture says about Lot.

Faith, instead, looks past what this world sees and finds a new world where God lives, where the ways of God are not our ways, nor do they make sense to us immediately. Faith believes the impossible. Faith accepts God's statements without criticism; what worldly knowledge can prove God wrong in what he says? Faith will go back to the story of Lot, certain that Peter was right, and start looking for proofs of Lot's righteousness instead of tripping over circumstances that could easily be interpreted either way.

Customs and culture

Remember that this story goes back 4000 years into a culture that we are strangers to. Not that God's rules of righteousness change from age to age, and are different from one culture to another; they don't and they aren't. But man changes very much, and when we read the stories of the Bible (especially of the Old Testament!) we are likely to miss the significance of what is going on, or get the wrong impression, simply because of the strangeness of the situation.

We simply can't understand the social customs of Lot's time by reading only the story in Genesis. The whole situation of Lot at the gate, welcoming the angels, them being in his home and eating with him, his reactions to the crowd gathering at his door –

there were customs going on here, that the story doesn't spell out in detail, that would explain the whole mystery of why each person did what he did if we knew what they were.

We blame Lot for settling down near Sodom, yet we forget that we also settle down near large towns and cities and take advantage of large groupings of people – how would we get along without electricity or transportation or grocery stores? We close our eyes to the sins of the wicked around us while taking advantage of the business and educational opportunities that being close to a city affords us. Is this a fault on our part? Or is this simply deciding on the level of comfort that we need in life and finding a way of fitting into one's culture to get it? How, then, is Lot blameworthy for the same thing?

Most modern American Christians don't believe in drinking wine, yet it was customary in Bible times to drink wine; it was usually the only thing to drink. Jesus drank wine! Yet modern students blame Lot for drinking (let's let alone, for now, how much he may have drunk!) as if that were sin on his part, as if it proved that he was an immoral character for turning to drink. We simply can't apply our modern standards to these early cultures!

There were other cultural forces at work in this story that we would do well to learn before we pass judgment on a world we don't immediately understand and we would never have fit into ourselves. It's not fair to blame someone back then for not living up to *our* standards; so let's be careful to use only God's eternal standards to judge someone by.

Jumping to conclusions

Another problem in interpreting the story of Lot is jumping to conclusions that aren't necessarily true. Too often we judge a situation before we find out all the facts; and once we have our conclusion, no amount of facts are going to change our minds!

For example, we assume that he failed to teach his family about God and didn't order his household in God's ways. The reason we assume this is because his wife and daughters turned out so badly! But is that the only explanation for this turn of events? Let's look at our own lives for the answer. Do all children of believers turn out to be believers themselves? If they don't, is that always the fault of the parents? The story of the prodigal son, by that false doctrine, should have been named the "failure of a dad" instead – he had two wayward sons!

Even the Law of God recognized that some children make a fateful decision: they decide that the faith of their parents isn't for them, and they turn away from it. The remedy was to stone the wayward son! (Deuteronomy 21:18-21) We can't prove that Lot failed in his duty; we can't prove that he put his business ahead of their spiritual condition. All we have are two facts: Peter claims he was righteous, and his family turned out wicked. What conclusions can we fairly draw from these facts alone?

Another false conclusion that students often draw from Lot's life is that he didn't mind living among the wicked Sodomites. Why else would he be there (instead of somewhere in Abraham's vicinity, for example) and why would he be on the town council? But again, we are assuming something that isn't true: we think that he winked at their wickedness in order to get along with them. But Peter boldly asserts the opposite: Lot was "distressed" at their wickedness. We are going to have to find another explanation for his being in the area; his feelings about their sin were holy and right.

Probably the biggest conclusion that people make about Lot is that he got what he deserved. How else can we explain the disasters that came upon him in his life? But this too is a false conclusion, based on assumptions that aren't true. We assume that those disasters were punishment for sin; but what sin was it a punishment of, if he was a "righteous" man as Peter claims? So we list his "sins" and show how they led to his downfall; but we will shortly look at those so-called sins and hopefully see that they weren't sins after all. Finally, were they punishments for sin? After looking at the passage in Peter, I'm not convinced that they were punishments – I'm more convinced that the punishments came on others, not on Lot, and that he escaped those disasters that others had to suffer. You see, it's all in how you look at it.

Start with false assumptions, and you'll arrive at the wrong conclusions; start with the truth, and you'll come to a different set of conclusions.

Is Lot the only sinner?

I'm reacting, I realize, to the sermons and lessons I've heard about Lot. But I have a feeling that the standard interpretation of the story of Lot is that he was a wretch who simply wouldn't live according to God's ways, so he paid the price. In fact, I have a feeling that most people, even when a little favorable to Peter's interpretation, will inevitably find something in Lot's life to condemn him for.

This reminds me of the old saying that people will tend to kick a man when he is down. There is something in human nature that likes to beat down the underdog. It doesn't matter how he got there – if he is down in the dust, he must deserve it! Somehow it makes us feel better. We end up kicking him even without good reason, as if we were more righteous than he is, as if we were his judges and are privileged to meet out justice to him.

But all good Christians realize that we are all guilty before God, that we are all sinners and deserving of his wrath and punishment. Only a fool depends on his own righteousness in the face of the holy God. That simply makes us the more pitiful looking when we viciously attack Lot for the very things that we ourselves do. Did Lot want to settle down in a nice area? So do we. Did Lot want to be near a city for the sake of making a better living? So do we. Did Lot live among a wicked people? So do we. Were Lot's family members unbelievers? So are ours. Was Lot taken advantage of, unknowingly by those he most depended on? So are we. So while we kick at Lot and accuse him of being a miserable spiritual failure, he writes our names in the dust (just as the Lord wrote the names of some Pharisees in the dust – John 8:1-11) as being no better off and having no better solutions to life's problems than he had.

Wasn't David an adulterer? Yet we give him more credit for being righteous than Lot, who would never do such a filthy thing. (Genesis 19:7) Didn't Peter deny Christ? Yet we accept him as a holy Apostle and call Lot a sinner, who welcomed God's angels into his house in spite of the trouble it would bring him. (Genesis 19:1-5) We are quick to forgive the sins of other saints in the Scriptures, but we are not willing to give the benefit of the doubt to Lot that he may have been a saint after all – in spite of the glowing report we get from Peter's testimony about him.

Of course this makes me suspicious that there is something going on here that most people are missing, or perhaps avoiding. My suspicion is that we are afraid of finding *ourselves* in the story of Lot – which leads me to the next point.

Lot: the picture of the modern Christian

My point is this: the story of Lot is the story of a believer living in a wicked world. This is *our* story; in fact, we can easier identify with Lot than with Abraham! The lesson from Lot is something that we, especially in our modern day, must learn or we will go down in disaster with the wicked culture that we are a part of.

166

We will see all the Scriptural elements of struggling with the world in the story of Lot. Jesus taught the same things that we learn from Lot, and the Apostles encouraged us with the story of Lot and others like him. The major Bible doctrines of sin are there, and of judgment, of salvation, of faith, of worship and duty toward God, of God's promises, of the trials and heartaches of mother against daughter and son against father, and "a man's enemies will be the members of his own household." (Matthew 10:36)

The thing about this story that caught my attention is that we also live in a wicked world, among wicked people, and struggle against social sins, and get hurt in the battle. The resemblance is too close to ignore. Other passages teach us this very thing, and we mustn't miss the significance: "Grace and peace to you from God our Father and the Lord Jesus Christ, who gave himself for our sins *to rescue us from the present evil age*, according to the will of our God and Father, to whom be glory for ever and ever." (Galatians 3:3-5) Don't be too quick to condemn Lot; rather, see yourself in his shoes and hope for the same God who rescued a helpless Lot to come and do the same for you.

Peter's View: the Controlling Passage

We mentioned earlier that, if it weren't for what Peter said about Lot, we probably would read the Genesis story with a much different viewpoint and draw different conclusions than we otherwise would. That makes Peter's account an important witness in this problem about Lot. In other words, before we close the book of Genesis and decide that we have the final interpretation on Lot, we must first listen to the Apostle's witness.

In fact, what we find in Peter is a paradox. We thought, after reading the Genesis story, that Lot was ungodly and wayward. Now Peter comes along and says the exact opposite! It makes us wonder if he has the same person in mind! Something is wrong: either Peter doesn't understand Lot, or we don't; but we have to solve the puzzle and get to the truth of the matter.

So we want to look at what Peter has to say and determine exactly what we must think about Lot. These kinds of problems in Scriptures are red flags, and we need to be careful when they happen. We can't simply ignore what Apostles have to say when they contradict our own opinions; we may not understand their point and our point may make more sense, but it's not good to challenge an Apostle! We must find out what the problem is and solve it so that our thinking fits in with the Spirit's thinking.

Here is the passage in Peter that we want to look at now:

For if God did not spare angels when they sinned, but sent them to Hell, putting them into gloomy dungeons to be held for judgment; if he did not spare the ancient world when he brought the flood on its ungodly people, but protected Noah, a preacher of righteousness,

168

and seven others; if he condemned the cities of Sodom and Gomorrah by burning them to ashes, and made them an example of what is going to happen to the ungodly; and if he rescued Lot, a righteous man, who was distressed by the filthy lives of lawless men (for that righteous man, living among them day after day, was tormented in his righteous soul by the lawless deeds he saw and heard) – if this is so, then the Lord knows how to rescue godly men from trials and to hold the unrighteous for the day of judgment, while continuing their punishment. (2 Peter 2:4-9)

A control

Peter's testimony is a control on the story of Lot. A *control* is a fact or situation that affects how we must think about another fact or situation. It's an unchangeable fact in itself, and well understood; and because it's there, it forces us to think a certain way about new facts that we don't understand yet. Scientists use controls many times during experiments, to help them understand what happens, and to keep themselves in line with knowledge they already have.

For example, a doctor wants to test a new drug. He doesn't know what it will do yet. So he divides a group of volunteers into two groups – the test group (who will take the drug) and the control group (who won't take the drug, but just a sugar pill instead.) He doesn't know yet what will happen with the test group, but he is absolutely certain about how the control group will act (in other words, *nothing* will happen to them – it's just a sugar pill). The differences between the two groups, then, he can assume came from the new drug.

Now let's apply the idea of a control to Bible study. Take two passages that talk about a subject. One passage is mysterious, confusing, open to different interpretations – if you read it with a certain point of view it seems to teach this, and from another point of view it could be teaching that. But the other passage – we aren't confused about that one at all. It's very clear, it leaves no room for various interpretations, it dictates what we must think about the subject. There is our control, that second passage. We understand it very well and we know what it's saying.

Now the purpose of the control passage is to help us understand the test passage. Take what you know to be true from the control passage and apply it to the confusing parts of the test passage. What we *know* will clear up what we *don't know*. And you certainly don't run this thing backwards! You can't let the confusing test passage convince you of things that contradict the control passage. You can't start with Genesis; instead you start with what Peter says, then move to the Genesis passage.

Peter knows something about Lot that we don't know; armed with this new knowledge, we must now return to the Genesis passage and re-read it, looking for evidence that Peter was right about Lot after all. We will find that the test passage suddenly takes on a different light, in view of the new facts.

Is this simply a way of making assumptions about the test passage that may not be true? No: the control passage is there for a reason; it didn't accidentally show up in Scripture. This is the way we *must* see the test passage if we want to know the truth about it. We aren't forcing false assumptions on the test passage when the control *tells* us to make those assumptions. The Lord gave us the control passage, in other words, so that we can understand the more difficult passage. Without the control we are lost.

Someone might ask, what about other passages that could be controls on the test passage? Well, that's good – you're thinking now about controls, and how important they are as tools in Bible study. But don't get carried away with controls or you are going to have them contradicting each other! One Bible study tool is just as important as the rest, but not to the exclusion of the rest. Keep in mind, in this subject of Lot, that the control passage tells us what to think *about Lot* – which is the whole problem. Other control passages deal with general subjects that may apply in ordinary circumstances; but this Peter passage gives the answer to the problem about Lot in particular. Therefore this control passage takes priority over others.

There are a couple of reasons why Peter is a control passage on the story of Lot. If you were simply taking my interpretation of the story, for example, you may have good reasons not to believe what I say! But Peter is an Apostle, sent by God with the eternal Truth, to enlighten the minds of ignorant men and bring them around to God's way of thinking. Now you just don't argue with an Apostle! His teaching is the foundation of the Church, the rock-basis (*especially* Peter – remember Jesus' prediction about him!) upon which the rest of the Church will see and know the true God. The Apostles played a unique role in the history of the Church (Ephesians 2:20); they will have an honored position in Heaven (Revelation 21:14), and they must be honored by Christians in this age for the part they have in building God's Kingdom. (Hebrews 2:1-4) The Lord Jesus had the words of life, and he passed those words on to his Apostles and made them stewards of the Truth. Whatever *our* opinions on the subject may be, only the Apostle is absolutely right.

Furthermore, this is the very Word of God, not simply the words of men. Paul claimed that authority when he wrote to the Thessalonians; he appreciated their response of faith when they heard his words:

And we also thank God continually because, when you received the Word of God, which you heard from us, you accepted it not as the word of men, *but as it actually is,*

the Word of God, which is at work in you who believe. (1
Thessalonians 2:13)

Peter himself says that the prophets spoke not their own
words but the words of the Spirit, as the Spirit moved them to
speak. (2 Peter 1:21) And Paul also taught that all Scripture is
"God-breathed" (2 Timothy 3:16) – in other words, coming from
God and not from man. This means, of course, that the facts in
Scripture are what God sees as the truth and must simply be
believed, not doubted or played with.

For these reasons, what Peter says about Lot is a control on
what to believe when we read Genesis. This is the truth, and this
is where we must start. Whatever we may find elsewhere in
Scripture, it must conform to what Peter teaches us.

Sterling character

Now let's move on to what Peter actually says about Lot.
Note his exact words:

Lot, a *righteous* man, who was distressed by the filthy
lives of lawless men (for that *righteous* man, living
among them day after day, was tormented in his *righteous*
soul by the lawless deeds he saw and heard) …

For the moment put aside what you read in Genesis and the
details that caused you problems. Assume that this is the first time
you've ever heard about the man Lot; let Peter introduce him to
you, and form your judgment of his character solely on the basis
of the Apostle's comments about him. What, from this passage
alone, do we learn about Lot?

For one thing, we find that he was a *righteous* man. That
word is used three times about Lot in one sentence. In fact, there
is nobody else in all of Scripture (except the Lord himself) that is

described in such glowing terms! *Nobody*. Peter seems to be beside himself as he packs in the descriptive words **righteous ... righteous ... righteous** in his one-sentence description of Lot.

This three-time emphasis is a technique that the Lord used in his Word to impress us with the truth of what he's talking about. It doesn't occur often, but when it does then we need to sit up and take notice. For example, in Isaiah we read that "Holy, holy, holy is the Lord Almighty." (Isaiah 6:3) The Lord should be able to say something once and we get it; when he says it three times, he wants to overwhelm us with this truth – he wants to get it into the most hardened heart and convince the most stubborn doubters. In other words, he isn't playing with us. So when he says that Lot was *righteous ... righteous ... righteous* – he means exactly what he says, in spite of what we think, and it's time to listen for a change.

What made Peter think so highly of Lot? We don't know, nor will we ever know until we get to Heaven and ask him. The Spirit obviously showed him something about Lot, something that convinced him that here was an amazingly righteous man, a man worthy to be used as a model for today's Christians, a true man of God.

But we shake our heads in disbelief. Peter, we answer, surely you must be mistaken about this guy. Haven't you read the story in Genesis? He did everything wrong! How can you say he was righteous, let alone use him as a model of righteousness? Couldn't you have picked someone else as a better example? David, for instance, or even Abraham from the same book?

But Peter insists on using Lot as his example. He passes by Abraham the man of faith and focuses on Lot (the more problematic of the two!) instead. This is very significant, because it was Abraham who was counted righteous and the father of the faithful! (Genesis 15:6) What does it means that Lot was

173

righteous? Knowing what other Scriptures say about it, a person is righteous because he has faith in God. (Romans 1:17; Romans 4; Hebrews 11:6) Therefore, Peter is telling us that Lot trusted in God and pleased him by obeying his commands. Are we stretching the point here, to make these kinds of assumptions about Lot? Not at all! The Bible is very plain about what God calls faith, what kind of behavior that he is pleased with, and who he is willing to reward with the title "righteous." When Lot is called *righteous ... righteous ... righteous*, then we can only assume that he excelled in the qualities that God looks for in a believer. The rest of Scripture won't let us assume anything else.

Not only does Peter call Lot righteous three times, he goes even farther and tells us what Lot thought of the people he lived around: "who was distressed by the filthy lives of lawless men ... was tormented in his righteous soul by the lawless deeds he saw and heard." In other words, he did *not* wink at their sin. If words mean anything at all, Lot had a righteous and holy attitude about the wickedness of Sodom. He hated it; it weighed heavily on his soul.

Sin is rebellion against God and his Law. Obviously the Sodomites had no regard for God; as it says in Romans 1, they were so far gone in their wickedness that God "gave them over to shameful lusts." (Romans 1:26) It must have been a spiritual nightmare.

But Lot demonstrated, by his utter horror of the wickedness of Sodom, a love for God and his commands. That's the point! You either love God and obey him, or you hate him and rebel against him. You either long to honor him or you find ways to shame him and his Creation. While the Sodomites struggled to erase the mark of God's Creation in their souls by searing their consciences and ruining each other, Lot would have been struggling to glorify God and remind them of his reality.

Are we assuming too much about Lot, to think that he maintained a high level of spiritual worship in his heart and life? Not at all! The Bible teaches plainly that only those who love God will be distressed at sin; only those who worship God and spend time in his presence will be tormented by the spiritual rebellion of those around him.

For, as I have often told you before and now say again *even with tears*, many live as enemies of the cross of Christ. Their destiny is destruction, their god is their stomach, and their glory is in their shame. Their mind is on earthly things. (Philippians 3:18-19)

As he approached Jerusalem and saw the city, *he wept over it* and said, "If you, even you, had only known on this day what would bring you peace – but now it is hidden from your eyes." (Luke 19:41-42)

Lot seems to be in good company, doesn't he? Only the best of God's people will weep over the sins of the wicked. Only the spiritual giants of the faith will agonize over the crimes of the wicked. Can we dare put Lot in this category? According to Peter, this was the kind of man he was.

The really pointed question to ask here, however, is this: What would *we* have done in his shoes? What if we were living in Sodom? Would we have kept our purity in such an environment? Would we have kept our faith in God, with nobody else around to be an encouragement to us? Who else could have lived in such a wicked place as Sodom and still be called, when it was all over, *a righteous man!*

Faith

When we have read what Peter has to say, and are convinced that this is God's opinion of Lot, the next step is the hardest one to take. We have to believe it.

"Faith comes from hearing the message, and the message is heard through the Word of Christ." (Romans 10:17) Faith happens after hearing what God has to say. He says the impossible, things contrary to human reason, what we would have least expected – but nevertheless it's truer than all of *our* judgments and opinions. He speaks because otherwise we would never know; it's a mercy that he tells us the truth! And faith is specially designed to take that truth of God, however unlikely and unlike what the world believes, and live by it.

Not everyone believes what God has to say, however. They see things the way the world sees things, and they don't know what it means to be led by the Spirit into the ways and world of God. They live by sight instead of by faith, in other words; they only know what their minds and senses tell them is most reasonable and true.

Now Christians have an important job to do. They are to learn the truth of God, get skilled in his ways that the Bible teaches them, and practice what they know in their daily lives. The key to all this, the beginning place of the entire process, is learning the truth: they must study the Word first before any of the rest will happen. And in order to truly understand what they read there, they have to approach it with faith that this is the way to look at things (not the way the world tells them) and this is what God wants us to build our lives upon. Even if they don't know *why* yet, they must trust God to know what he is doing. It will become plainer as time goes on and as they use the truth that God gives them.

Peter wants us to go back to the story of Lot and re-read it. He must have had a feeling that people would misinterpret the story (maybe he did himself before the Spirit taught him!) and he doesn't want us to miss out on something. There is something in this story of Lot that we must learn! That's the only explanation for Peter making such a fuss about a character that we were ready to write off as a failure.

But in order to go back to that story, we must take faith with us and be armed with a few facts that God will reveal to us. Without faith, and without the testimony of Peter, we certainly can't get anything different than what everyone else gets from the story. But with faith in God's Word and trust that the Lord knows what he is doing, we are going to get an entirely different picture of Lot than what others see. Some Scriptures require some faith to get the point, others require a great deal of faith; this one is one of the latter kind.

But then that's been true of the Bible since its beginning. Jesus pointed out to the Jews that they had been reading the Scriptures for centuries and they never saw Christ in them, even though he is all through the book. (John 5:39-40) Unless Paul had pointed out some critical doctrines in the Old Testament we would have missed them entirely – like Abraham being the father of all the faithful, Jew and Gentile alike, and Sarah and Hagar being like Heaven and the earthly Jerusalem. In mercy God has provided all these clues to enable us to go back and re-read the old stories, seeing them in a different light, finding life and hope in them instead of dullness and deadness.

Peter's point

It seems that when a preacher or teacher starts some lessons on Lot, they follow a standard procedure. First they list the things that Lot did, and then allegorize them so that he turns out to be a spiritual scoundrel, always choosing the world instead of God's treasures, and then they point out the failures in his life that we could have predicted. This outline must be written in some seminary textbook somewhere, for as faithfully as most teachers follow it!

But Peter gives us a different sermon outline, a different point to make about the story of Lot. When Peter looks at the life of Lot, this is what he sees: *Amazing rescues!* "... and if he *rescued* Lot ... then the Lord knows how to *rescue* godly men from trials and to hold the unrighteous for the day of judgment while continuing their punishment." (2 Peter 2:7,9)

In other words, he does *not* see an allegory here. An allegory is a story on a physical level with a totally spiritual meaning. For example, Paul says that the story about Sarah and Hagar represents Heaven (Sarah) and earthly Jerusalem (Hagar). (Galatians 4:21-31) Now when an Apostle tells us that a story is an allegory, *then* we have the freedom to interpret it that way; they know what they are talking about. But Bible students soon start seeing allegories all over the Bible when there is no need to or, what is worse, when the text just doesn't teach that. Probably the single worst error they commit in this story of Lot is to turn it into an allegory: Sodom is the world, Lot is a lukewarm Christian, and the point is to *separate oneself from the world!* But that's *not* what Peter sees! To him, the story isn't an allegory; the point to him is that God can rescue his people from even the worst situations. Isn't that what he says about it?

What impresses Peter the most about Lot was the way the Lord rescued him from many potential disasters. The first one was the time the foreign kings defeated Sodom and carried Lot and his family away. Abraham came to the rescue (with just 318 men!) and rescued Lot and all that were with him. The second rescue is more subtle but perhaps even more miraculous: the Lord rescued Lot spiritually from the wickedness that gripped Sodom, down to the last man. There were not even ten righteous people in the entire city! (Genesis 18:32) Yet in the face of the incredible pressure of wickedness and potential persecution, Lot maintained his spiritual integrity to the point that Peter called him *righteous ... righteous ... righteous*. The third rescue, obviously, was the time the angels came in after him and got him out before the Lord destroyed Sodom.

What happened to everyone else? The Sodomites were defeated and killed in battle, they succumbed to unbelievable sin and destroyed themselves morally and physically, they lay helpless under the fiery judgment from the skies that God rained down on them, Lot's sons-in-law died right along with the Sodomites, Lot's wife disobeyed the Lord and died instantly, Lot's daughters committed incest – Lot was the only one who survived the whole crazy thing intact! Everyone else around him was falling like flies *and he alone escaped!*

He who dwells in the shelter of the Most High will rest in the shadow of the Almighty. I will say of the LORD, "He is my refugee and my fortress, my God, in whom I trust." Surely he will save you from the fowler's snare and from the deadly pestilence. He will cover you with his feathers, and under his wings you will find refuge, his faithfulness will be your shield and rampart. You will not fear the terror of night, nor the arrow that flies by day, nor the pestilence that stalks in the darkness, nor the plague that destroys at midday. A thousand may fall at your side, ten thousand at your right hand, but it will not come near you. You will only observe with your eyes and see the punishment of the wicked. If you make the Most High your dwelling – even the LORD, who is my refuge – then no harm will befall you, no disaster will come near your tent. For he will command his angels concerning you to guard you in all your ways; they will lift you up in their hands, so that you will not strike your foot against a stone.

You will tread upon the lion and the cobra; you will trample the great lion and the serpent. "Because he loves me," says the LORD, "I will rescue him; I will protect him, for he acknowledges my name. He will call upon me, and I will answer him; I will be with him in trouble, I will deliver him and honor him. With long life will I satisfy him and show him my salvation." (Psalm 91)

If you look at the life of Lot from *this* angle, can you think of anybody in Scripture that is such a good example of what this Psalm teaches? You may answer, "But look at the misery Lot had along the way! Is this the Lord's salvation?" But the Lord never promised laughs and good times; he did predict that "in this world you *will* have trouble." (John 16:33) We *are* going to have burdens and trials the whole way. But when destruction comes – either from sin and its effects or from God's judgments – he will snatch us up out of the way and the wicked will go through it without us. We will be safe in the Lord's hands. That's a principle we find throughout the Bible. And Peter was impressed so much with how the Lord rescued Lot over and over that he made it the point of this passage.

Now why don't we see the same thing? Why do our lessons on Lot focus on Lot the sinner, yet Peter's lesson focuses on God rescuing righteous Lot from disaster? On one side of the street you have some preacher pounding the pulpit, condemning Lot for everything he did. On the other side in another church you have the Apostle Peter preaching the amazing salvation of God, using Lot as an object lesson. It's startling how different these two points are! It leads me to believe that something is wrong in our world view, that there are certain flaws in our system of beliefs that prevent us from seeing the truth about God and his works. One flaw, I believe, is that modern Christians don't like the picture of God sending his wrath on anybody, no matter how much they might have deserved it! And they also

180

don't believe strongly enough that God saves those he sets his love on (not because they deserve anything from him) or that he is able to keep them from falling along the way. There may be other flaws in our thinking as well, but these two are fatal enough.

Now what?

Now we must return to the story of Lot and re-read it. This time we are going to be sensitive to what Peter said about the man, and look for good things instead of bad things. This isn't putting blinders on, either, because now we have reason to believe that Lot was more righteous than we gave him credit for. We had blinders on before now, when we were looking for sin in Lot's life. Peter, however, has corrected our thinking and we hopefully will see what is actually there in the text instead of what we wanted to see there.

The Story of Lot Examined

Let's look at the story of Lot now very carefully, looking for things that will support Peter's view. Not that we are going to be dishonest with the text; on the contrary, we want to be very fair with the text. The problem about many passages of Scripture is that they can be looked at from different directions and made to say different things, so much so that one would think that some of the interpretations we hear have come from different Bibles!

But the Bible only has one meaning, it has many applications. The story of Lot only has one meaning; what we have to do is use Peter's clues on how to read it, so that we get that one true meaning. God is not a God of confusion but a God of truth. He wants us to get the point, whatever it is, and then get busy building it into our lives to become more profitable servants.

Abraham and Lot separate

In Genesis 13 we read about Abraham and Lot moving away from each other. Read that chapter carefully and then note the following things about it:

- *Lot knew about Abraham's God:* We first read about Lot in Genesis 11, when he set out with his uncle Abraham from Ur and traveled west. At Haran a large part of the clan settled down, but Abraham and Lot went on to the land of Canaan because of the promise of God. Does this tell you anything about Lot's hopes and faith?

  Lot was with Abraham from his calling all the way up to the initial tour through Canaan, the trip to Egypt, and then back again to Canaan. He was with Abraham when he twice built an altar to worship God, and another time when it says that Abraham "called on the name of the LORD." (Genesis 13:4) We aren't told of anybody else of Abraham's immediate family who was with him during these travels, and nobody else seemed interested in Abraham's God, except Lot. I believe we can safely assume that he not only knew about the God of Abraham, he was ready and willing to follow the Lord, with his uncle, into this new land and life.

- *He was still new to the area:* Notice when the separation occurred: they had just come *through Canaan* for the first time, on a tour you might say, looking over the place. They did not travel by way of Sodom, remember; it says that they went through Canaan. Then they went on to Egypt, because of the famine. Right after they came back from Egypt they separated to their own ways. There is no reason to believe that Lot knew much about the local peoples and the extent of their wickedness. The writer of Genesis knew (after the fact), and we know, but Lot didn't necessarily know. When he chose the land around Sodom to settle down, all he might have known about them was that they were about the same as the Canaanites (who, we might add, were very wicked people in their own right, and Abraham lived among *them*!). Put yourself in his shoes: do you know everything about your neighbors when you move to a new neighborhood? Especially when you are from out of town? Of course not! They aren't going to come out and tell you right away how wicked they are!

- *They had to do something:* The story makes it plain that something had to be done. Abraham and all his people, and Lot and all his people, simply couldn't coexist in the same area anymore. "But the land could not support them while they stayed together, for their possessions were so great that they were not able to stay together." (Genesis 13:6) This isn't condemning anybody; it's just a fact. Their herds probably numbered in the upper thousands, and you need a certain amount of grassland to take care of all those animals. The argument that Lot should have stayed with Abraham doesn't hold water; it just wasn't possible anymore.

- *Abraham suggested the split:* Notice who made the suggestion that they part company. It wasn't Lot's idea! Abraham was the head of the clan, and Lot would have submitted to his elder's decisions – even if Abraham was gracious enough to "discuss" it with his nephew. Abraham, in effect, sent his nephew away. If anybody has to take the blame for what happened to Lot, perhaps we need to look to his uncle!

We mustn't forget how society worked in those days. The oldest male member of a family clan was the highest authority. Survival was hard enough in those days; the importance of a chain of command can't be emphasized enough. Abraham's "suggestion" meant that something, in his opinion, had to be done, and Lot (regardless of whether he wanted to go) did what his uncle wanted out of respect for the elder man.

Besides, Lot wasn't moving away from covenant protection. That viewpoint simply ignores the rest of the story! Abraham both rescued him and prayed on his behalf. The Lord's protection very definitely covered Lot in all his troubles.

- *Where was this place?* Scholars just aren't sure where Sodom was located. There are two possibilities: on the north end of the Dead Sea, or on the south end. Here is a rough map of the area:

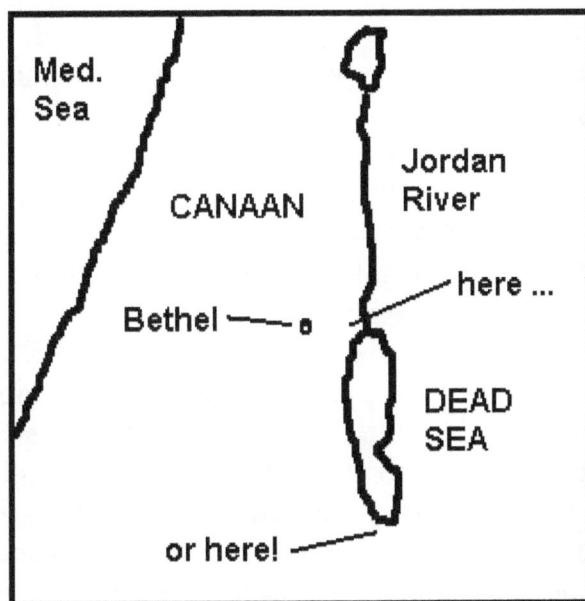

Possible locations for Sodom

I realize that's quite a range, but there are good arguments for either place. For instance, the tar pits that Genesis 14:10 mentions are located on the south end of the Dead Sea; that's one argument. But it doesn't say that Sodom was located there – it only says that the battle occurred there. On the other hand, Abraham "looked down toward Sodom and Gomorrah" and saw them burning. (Genesis 19:28) You can't see to the south end of the Dead Sea from where Abraham was standing, which is near Bethel in the mountains above Jericho.

Wherever the city was located, it was within range of Abraham's watchful eye – which Lot had plenty of reason to be thankful for!

- *New neighbors:* As we saw above, it's not fair to Lot to accuse him of purposely closing his eyes to the wickedness of the Sodomites for the sake of improving his business possibilities. Although the text says, "Now the men of Sodom were wicked and were sinning greatly against the LORD" (Genesis 13:13), that doesn't necessarily mean that Lot or Abraham knew that. Don't you think that Abraham would have had something to say to his nephew (for whom he felt responsible, as we will see when the story unfolds) about moving to such a place – if they would have known?

  We know they were wicked – but then we are after the fact. So was the writer of the book of Genesis. But Lot was a newcomer to the area and probably didn't hear much about what they were like, especially since he was a wanderer with Abraham and didn't get a chance to lean over some fence and chat with the neighbors. And when he moved there, he certainly would have begun to see their sin – but probably not on moving day, since, at first, people like to put on a good show to each other. Their bodies didn't appear as monsters, you know! They looked just like people that you and I know. Wicked hearts show up in the behavior, and *that* is only seen over time.

- *Chose a good land:* "Lot looked up and saw that the whole plain of the Jordan was well watered, like the garden of the LORD, like the land of Egypt, toward Zoar." (Genesis 13 :10) Remember that he had just come back from Egypt (after seeing the Nile River and its irrigation systems). After wandering through some pretty bleak country (the Negev was desert) the sight of good pasture and plenty of water must have impressed him.

There is nothing wrong with wanting a nice place to live! People jump on Lot for making this choice, as if he was supposed to pick a more difficult and forlorn place to live! Look at the possibilities: either he could choose Canaan, which was mountainous (he just traveled through the length of it) and full of wary and antagonistic Canaanites who were sitting on the good pasture land (Genesis 13:7); or he could choose the plain along the Jordan River, which was flat and made up of rich grasslands, and had plenty of elbow room for everybody. He made the natural choice, the one we all would have made in his place. We make that same kind of decision many times in our own lives as we choose jobs, neighborhoods, schools, friends, hobbies, entertainment, and so on.

The point of this story isn't the fact that he chose the wrong place to live because of his greed. The point is that even though a place looks good, there may very well be trouble lurking there, unknown to the chooser. Of course this was true about the area around Sodom. Should he have known about Sodom? Not reasonably. So instead of blaming him, we need to be looking for a hidden agenda in the writer's mind.

- ***This was covenant land too:*** Did you know that this entire area was part of the land that the Lord promised to give Abraham and his seed? Lot wasn't moving out of Abraham's jurisdiction; he was moving to the eastern end of the covenant land! Notice the promise that comes again to Abraham: "Lift up your eyes from where you are and look north and south, ***east*** and west. All the land that you see I will give to you and your offspring forever." (Genesis 13:14- 15) Lot moved east; the Lord promised that to Abraham also. If you remember when the twelve tribes returned from Egypt and where they settled, you

187

will know that the land where Lot lived was settled by Judah and Benjamin on the west and north of the Dead Sea, and Reuben on the east side. The whole area belonged to Abraham! Abraham got the land "flowing with milk and honey" (Deuteronomy 6:3) and Lot got the land "well watered like the garden of the LORD." I don't see where Lot was doing anything wrong.

- ***Set-up for a rescue, not a statement on sin:*** As we saw above, the writer is obviously setting up something here. Although the land looks good, there is trouble here – unknown to these two newcomers. Notice how he puts together the pieces of the picture: Abraham needs room and sends Lot away; Lot picks, ironically, the very spot where there will be trouble; Abraham is going to have to come rescue his nephew soon. The story is set up for a rescue; it's not an examination of Lot's heart and motives. To get the point of the passage you have to back up and see the whole picture, the whole context, especially in light of what happens before and after the story.

The rescue from the kings

In Genesis 14 we read the story about Lot being taken captive, and Abraham rescuing him from his captors. The story line is this: the king of Sodom and several other kings decided that they didn't want to pay tribute anymore to the kings who held the power over this area of the country – Kedorlaomer and his gang – so they rebelled. The four ruling kings decided to come out and teach the Sodomites a lesson. They met near the tar pits of the Dead Sea, where many of the Sodomite army got stuck and killed. The king of Sodom and his allies, of course, lost the battle, but many escaped with their lives.

Lot, unfortunately, was right in the way of the battle and the victorious kings picked him up and took him along, with all his people and possessions. Abraham, when told of what had happened to his nephew, set off with a band of his own men (318) in hot pursuit. They caught up with Kedorlaomer and his gang, drove them away, and returned Lot and his possessions safely home. There is the additional story of the king of Salem – Melchizedek – to whom Abraham gave a tithe of everything he picked up in the rescue. When the king of Sodom offered to reward Abraham for his act of heroism, Abraham refused to take anything from him, saying he didn't want to be accused of becoming rich at Sodom's expense.

There's the story. It's about a rescue, about people in trouble and a concerned relative successfully getting them out of trouble. It happened all the time back then. Yet people have found things to blame Lot for in this story too! Let's look at some of the details and see if we can learn what actually happened:

- ***This happened all the time:*** Life was cruel and harsh in those days, a fact that we modern Americans don't often consider when reading these stories. Bands of thieves and roving armies made constant raids throughout the countryside; it was common for people who didn't get to protection in time to get completely wiped out. Remember there was no United Nations to punish those marauders! They simply raped, robbed and murdered at will and then went away, if they got away with it. Most people lived behind stout city walls, because it would be suicide to live outside the walls, given the situation. You really ought to pick up a history of the Ancient Near East and do a little reading on what life was like in those days, if for no other reason than to appreciate your life of ease today.

Was Lot inside the city of Sodom when this battle happened? We don't know. But even those inside the city were taken captive by Kedorlaomer and his allies. Their fate, according to how things went in those days, was this:

the women (married and unmarried) would become concubines for the victorious soldiers; the children may or may not be spared to live as slaves, and the men (those who weren't killed because of being potential threats to the captors) would be sold as slaves to surrounding kingdoms. This happened if the raiders were feeling particularly good that day! Otherwise nothing breathing would survive, they would all be put to death, left to rot on the ground, and only their possessions would be taken. It was a rough world.

So we can't blame Lot for living so close to danger. Wherever he lived, he would have been exposed to this kind of thing. The whole country was full of roving bands doing particularly horrible things to whoever didn't have exceptional defenses in place. So the writer of the story isn't showing us how Lot was getting his due, sinner as he was; we are missing the point if that's what we get out of it. Rather we learn about how Lot was rescued from something that many people had to go through in those days, and what most people didn't escape from alive.

- *An innocent bystander:* There is absolutely no mention of any good reason why Lot would have been picked on by the invading armies, other than he happened to be in the way. So the point isn't that he should have stayed away from Sodom; what it's addressing is that we often get into trouble unjustly in this world – and what are we going to do when that happens?

- *A miracle:* One important point to remember about culture in those days was that "kingdoms" were usually pretty small. When someone was called a "king," that may have meant no more than he was the head man of a small town; his "kingdom" extended around the town, including

190

the farmland that the townspeople worked, for only a few square miles. It was a rare kingdom that was large enough to impress us moderns.

In this instance four kings got together for a raid, and after terrorizing the neighborhood first they then turned their attention to the kingdom of Sodom and its allies. We aren't talking about millions of men here. A few thousands, probably, at the most. But they were enough to successfully accomplish all they had set out to do.

Abraham, however, only had 318 men on his side. He followed them north, caught them where Dan is located, and in the middle of the night attacked and sent the enemy running. So even though he had a smaller force, through persistence and surprise he won the encounter and rescued Lot.

I believe we have good reason for saying, however, that under normal circumstances such a rescue was highly unlikely. First of all, Kedorlaomer certainly had more than 300 men on his side! He couldn't have pulled off the entire campaign with a tiny force. Second, the text says that *the Lord* won this battle:

> Blessed be Abram by God Most High,
> Creator of Heaven and earth.
> And blessed be God Most High,
> who delivered your enemies into your hand.
> (Genesis 14:19-20)

The credit for the victory went to God, not to Abraham. We give God credit for things because he can do what we can't do on our own; that's why we need him. This is what we call a "miracle", when God steps in and does something contrary to normal circumstances.

Scripture enjoys showing God off, so to speak. It tells us stories of the Lord's victories, how he wins the battle through his amazing strength and overpowering wisdom. It takes all the opportunities available to "glorify" the Lord so that we will learn who this God is that we follow. Don't miss the point! The Bible is again teaching us about God in this story of the rescue of Lot, not sub-plots that we think we can find if we look hard enough between the lines.

For instance, it shows us that God uses only a few to do his work, and they always succeed because he fights for them. (A principle that is well-developed in other stories throughout the Bible.) It teaches us that God takes care of his own; he cares for them, and through his servants he will rescue them. It teaches us the doctrine of rescue (or deliverance), one of the main themes of the entire Bible (study this out!) which is what his people are constantly in need of. We could go on, but I'll let you look for God in this passage. You miss the point of Scripture if you don't see God in every story.

- *The responsibility of the clan leader:* The reason that Abraham went after Lot was because of his responsibilities as leader of the clan; he was the oldest male member, and therefore the "boss" and spiritual head over the entire family. It didn't matter that they split up earlier; Abraham still had a responsibility to take care of his nephew when necessary.

- *Notice who did the rescue:* A further dimension in this story is something that we mustn't forget or fail to appreciate. Abraham was the father of the faithful, the receiver of the Covenant, the spiritual head of his family.

It was through him that the Lord would bless his people. Here is an instance of that promise at work. God promised Abraham that "All the peoples on earth will be blessed through you" (Genesis 12:3), and he is going to start in his own family. So it's a mistake to focus on Lot's troubles here; we all have troubles! "In this world you will have trouble." (John 16:33) But who is so fortunate as to have an uncle Abraham, a favorite of God, to rescue them from that trouble? Not many. "But take heart! I have overcome the world." That, I believe, is the point of this story. All the other details support that point.

The rescue from Sodom

Now we move to another rescue. Before the actual deliverance takes place, however, we are allowed into God's war council – the war preparations before the battle. In Genesis 18 we read about three angels who visit Abraham: first to promise him a son (Genesis 18:1-15) and then to talk about the problem of Sodom. (Genesis 18:16-33)

There are two important elements in this story that we must look at. First, Abraham prays for the righteous of the city. It's not Sodom itself that he's concerned about, but the righteous who are living there.

Will you sweep away the righteous with the wicked? What if there are fifty righteous people in the city? Will you really sweep it away and not spare the place for the sake of the fifty righteous people in it? Far be it from you to do such a thing – to kill the righteous with the wicked, treating the righteous and the wicked alike. Far be it from you! Will not the Judge of all the earth do right? (Genesis 18:23-25)

There's no question that the Lord will do the right thing; he doesn't treat the righteous like the wicked, and he will rescue the righteous from disaster. The story that follows this discussion proves that point. The question is this, however: *are* there any righteous people living in Sodom? Will the Lord find at least ten righteous people in Sodom? Who are the righteous?

Remember that this is Abraham asking this question, the man who was counted righteous because of his faith. (Genesis 15:6) He understands what righteousness is all about. So he is asking the Lord for a head count, so to speak, a census of people who may be living in Sodom with a righteousness beyond what this world counts as "goodness" – a living faith in the true God, resting in his Word, following him in all his will. The quest is on, and the angels will go to Sodom to see if there are any people living there with this kind of righteousness.

Second, Abraham is doing his covenant thing. He really set the Lord up with this question! Who else but Lot would have this kind of righteousness? Perhaps he was hoping that Lot would have been able to influence other Sodomites to believe in God, and so by now there would be ten righteous people living there. Whatever may have happened, Abraham knew Lot would qualify, and he was concerned for his safety in case the Lord destroyed Sodom. In other words, he was doing his covenant duty – being father of the faithful, getting blessings from God for the benefit of his spiritual family. Isn't it true that the "prayer of a righteous man is powerful and effective"? (James 5:16) Especially *this* righteous man! This ought to remind us of Moses, who often stood in the gap for the people of Israel and got God's blessings for them.

Now let's look at the elements of the story recorded in chapter 19 and learn more about Lot and his behavior:

- ***The search of the two angels:*** We have to keep in mind what these two angels are here for. They are looking for righteous people: if they find, according to the discussion with Abraham, at least ten righteous people in Sodom then they won't destroy the city. They aren't going to be impressed with low-level definitions of righteousness, either! This is God's special work, this business of judgment, and he is going to find those who are really righteous. "Man looks at the outward appearance, but the LORD looks at the heart." (1 Samuel 16:7)

   Angels also have another purpose. The name "angel" means "messenger", and in this case they have two messages to deliver from the Lord: one to Lot, to flee from the wrath to come, and one to Sodom, a message of death.

- ***Lot sitting in the gateway:*** It's true that the elders of a city sat in the gate in those days, and there is where the current events were discussed and problems solved. Just by him being there, we get the idea that Lot was important enough to the people of the city to be wanted in on the discussions. It doesn't tell us anything about his intentions, however.

   Don't we have Christians in our government? Do they necessarily agree with the wickedness that goes on there, even the wicked decisions that are made? Just by being involved in government functions doesn't mean that they agree with everything that happens! We can't accuse Lot, either, of being so wrapped up in the affairs of Sodom that he couldn't discern their wickedness, that he actually approved of their behavior. Just the bare fact of his being in on the governing body doesn't tell us a thing about his thoughts.

We have to surmise his intentions from what we know about him, not from conclusions that we may jump to when we see him sitting there at the gate. If he was a *righteous ... righteous ... righteous* man, and if he was under the covenant of God (which we've seen proof of already), what can we safely assume about his involvement with the Sodomites? Only this: he was probably the only good influence on the city council! If he was truly distressed at the wickedness of the city, would you be impressed to find him trying to counter-act that wickedness? In fact, wouldn't you expect that from a righteous man? Although the story doesn't tell us what he was doing there, knowing his character would lead us to believe that he was doing all he could to influence events for the better. In fact, we do see him doing just that, later in the story – Genesis 19:7-8. He never was considered one of them (as we see in their remark in Genesis 19:9), so his being around them must have been a matter of his intentions to change *them* rather than them appreciating him.

- *Welcoming the angels:* We too easily miss the significance of this part of the story. In those days it was an unwritten social rule that you should welcome strangers into your home. There were no hotels or motels, and travel was long, tedious, difficult and expensive. It was considered nothing short of rudeness to refuse a passing traveler food and rest; later the Law of Moses would make provision for taking care of passers-by. (Deuteronomy 10:18, Matthew 25:35) In other words, this was a test of character: how do people treat others in their need?

If nobody offered a stranger a place to stay for the night, they would have to stay in the town square all night, perhaps cold and hungry, and they would inevitably pass on a bad report to other cities and travelers about this inhospitable place they met with on their travels. At the very least that meant that the city's business would drop off as a result; at the most, as in this case with Sodom, it would mean their lives!

Notice who offered the strangers a meal and bed! Lot immediately responded to their needs; he was the only one to do so. According to the Law of God, here was a righteous man; his actions proved the condition of his heart.

- ***The meal he prepared:*** The Hebrew word is "feast" – he really went all out to entertain his guests. When you do this for someone, you are showing them how special they are to you. Did he know that they were angels sent by God? Probably not, since they didn't reveal themselves to him until later in the story. But Lot is doing something that few people are willing to do. He is spending his wealth and time on men he doesn't even know. How many people do you know who would spend their time and money on even their relatives, let alone perfect strangers! Yet this is a mark of a righteous man, that he extends his help willingly to those in need. (Matthew 25:34-40)

Besides, Lot may have discerned these men's righteousness – he probably did! – and it was a breath of fresh air to entertain good men for a change. Being distressed at the Sodomites' constant wickedness more than likely made Lot all the more enthusiastic about spending the night in the company of men who understood the fear of the Lord; he no doubt looked forward to hours of holy and wholesome conversation with them.

Notice, however, that he did the very same thing that his uncle Abraham did just days before this: these very same angels showed up at Abraham's tent, and he too went all out to feed them and make them comfortable. Isn't it remarkable that the very law that proves that a man is righteous is done both by the father of the faithful and his nephew? Can we draw conclusions about how much like Abraham that Lot is?

There is one more fascinating tidbit about this meal. Notice what he served them: unleavened bread. This is not something that we would have expected to see, long before the story of Passover and unleavened bread; yet it's highly significant in the context of the entire Bible. It was very appropriate to serve these angels bread without yeast since it was the symbol of redeemed Israel and a life without sin (as Jesus explains in Matthew 16:12 and Paul explains in 1 Corinthians 5:6-8). Somehow Lot was enabled to see the symbol of holiness, of not being saturated with sin like the Sodomites, of presenting to God an acceptable sacrifice of a holy and clean life. This is the kind of thing the angels were looking for.

- *All the men of the city:* Here is how verse 4 reads in the Hebrew original: "The men of the city ... the men of Sodom ... both young and old ... all of the people ... to the last man." We get the idea that the writer wants us to know that *all* the men of the city came out and surrounded Lot's house! There is a reason for this, of course: the angels came to see if there were any righteous men in the city, and here they are presenting themselves for inspection! It will be an easy matter to look over the crowd and pick out the righteous ones; all they had to do was count heads and see if they could find at least ten.

Notice too how the count went. All those outside the house (the entire city) were demanding the right to commit wickedness. And all those inside the house (Lot) were appalled at such wickedness. The angels didn't have to spend much time figuring out the situation.

- *Lot and the crowd:* In Hebrew it says that he called them "my brothers," which naturally distresses us because we hate to hear him call them this. But it may be nothing more than the proverb of "turning away wrath" with a gentle answer; he was appealing to them as fellow citizens, in a way that should remind them of his sitting with them at the gate and helping them to see God's ways and give up their wickedness. There's nothing wrong with being politic in a volatile situation.

What is interesting, however, is the fact that he closed the door behind him when he went out to address the crowd. This is just a little icing on the cake that showed Lot's heart. He was too embarrassed over the open immorality of the Sodomites to let his guests see or hear what was going on; he took the sordid job upon himself and tried to insulate his guests from the wickedness. He, of course, thought that they couldn't hear; but they, being angels, knew what he was going through on their behalf outside the door. It's a good thing they could hear through walls!

- *Offering his two daughters:* Up until this part of the story Lot has done absolutely nothing that can even be construed into something wrong. Now, however, we run into a hitch. Why in the world did he offer his two daughters to the crowd, to "do what you like with them" (Genesis 19:8)?

Let's analyze the situation, keeping in mind Lot's performance up until this point. **First**, this was an extremely dangerous and touchy situation. The men of Sodom were about to do something, there was no mistaking that. Lot had seen enough of their behavior in the past that he was alarmed at what was about to happen. At a time of crisis like this, anything could happen, people lose their heads, and it is extremely difficult to do the right thing – there isn't much time to think.

Second, the rules of social behavior dictated that Lot protect these strangers with his life. Being a righteous man, he would have spent the rest of his days in infamy if he would have let the Sodomites molest the guests in his house. (Genesis 19:8) We underestimate the strength of this unspoken principle in their society; we don't really have anything that corresponds to it in ours, being individualistic as we are and having ready recourse to police and courts and insurance claims. And perhaps we would have done differently, stepping aside and allowing the crowd to do what they wanted with people we don't really know and care little for, but Lot just couldn't do that to these holy men. Lot was, literally, their only protection as their host.

Third, he at least offered a better solution than what they were demanding! It would have been bad enough for them to have his daughters; it was unthinkable, however, if they would have committed homosexuality. These Sodomites were not only wicked, they were *unnaturally* wicked – as Paul describes in Romans 1. Such things shouldn't even be mentioned, let alone done! Sex is something between man and woman, not between man and man. This, I believe, is what Lot's point was here. Love for family took second place to love for God's Law. I'm afraid that we don't have many people of that spiritual caliber today even among dedicated Christians. Lot was willing to give up his most precious possessions for the sake of God's righteousness.

Given the circumstances, then, we can say this at least: it was a crisis, and it's difficult to be cool, calm and collected in such a situation. And the Sodomites were obviously going to do something. If Lot couldn't protect his family, he at least could make a statement about God's Law, which is a higher standard in life and must not be violated at all costs, even at the cost of his family.

When the angels saw that he was ready to give up his family for their sake, they immediately pulled him inside and revealed their plans to him. This incident makes me think that they felt they had finally found their righteous man.

Finally, wasn't Abraham called upon to put his son to death? And if God would not have stopped him, he would have plunged his knife into Isaac's throat and we moderns would have been horrified! The parallel is too significant to ignore here: many things that the elder does, the nephew also does, although in different forms. They must have had the *same faith*, in other words.

• *The testing of Lot:* The first third of this passage describes how the angels tested Lot. Remember from Genesis 18:16-33 that the Lord promised, because Abraham pressed him for the promise, that he wouldn't destroy the city of Sodom if there were ten righteous people in it. So before the angels can do the work of punishment, they have to find the righteous people.

Lot immediately showed his colors when they arrived in town. When he insisted that they stay at his house, despite their protests to the contrary and in spite of the fact that it might bring trouble to him, he scored one point – a righteous man does such things for travelers and strangers. The meal was the second point scored: it was an amazing act of faith for Lot to serve these angels (still unknown to him) unleavened bread. It was an appropriate thing to do, in light of the fact that they were looking for *holy* men, and leaven is the Bible's symbol of wickedness.

He scored another point when he put himself between the wicked men of Sodom and the strangers. Not only was it a courageous thing to do, but custom demanded that a host do whatever necessary to protect his guests. Since the Sodomites wanted to commit sexual immorality with the angels, Lot showed his colors again in refusing them any opportunity for such wickedness.

It was then that the angels were satisfied that they had a righteous man on their hands. But notice how they determined all this: they watched Lot's *actions*. They could see that he did righteous things, and they could also see that his faith motivated him to do these righteous things. His faith overruled his fear. It was obvious that Lot believed in God in such a way that it moved him to do those things which most pleased God, even though he may not have been aware of the fact he was being watched. This is a good example of what the Apostle talks about in James 2:14-26.

- *Lot's family problems:* He certainly had these! As the story progresses we are amazed at how his whole family turned out so badly. Poor Lot struggled all along with family problems, as if he needed this extra burden when he had to deal with the Sodomites. There have been many who faulted Lot for how badly his family turned out – his sons-in-law refused to leave the city with him, his wife loved the city too much to leave it, his daughters committed incest with their father. It's easy to blame him for not instructing them in the ways of the Lord.

But it may not be all his fault. We don't have the license to assume that Lot didn't train them in the ways of the Lord; does it *say* that about him? Since Peter calls him a righteous man, can we fairly assume that in this area he was unrighteous? Because they turned out badly, is that reason to assume that he failed them? Aren't there other alternatives?

> A man's enemies will be the members of his own household. (Matthew 10:36)

It's entirely possible that he did try to instruct them. His sons-in-law would take their own counsel and not necessarily feel obligated to listen to him. His wife, as many people in history can testify to, decided for herself what she wanted in life, and she obviously didn't share her husband's view on things. It's unfortunate but true that many families are divided when it comes to the things of the Lord, through nobody's fault in particular. His daughters – well, we will look at their story in a minute; but we can safely assume that they learned their ways from their wicked neighbors. Children don't always turn out right, in spite of all efforts to the contrary.

It could very well be that Lot was the only righteous person in Sodom! This story isn't making a statement about Lot's style in conducting his family affairs; it's simply showing you who are the righteous and who are the wicked. You would miss its point if you pushed it further than that. How these people came to be wicked, we can only guess, but we *know* that Lot is not one of them. Just remember that you and I are in the same boat – we are surrounded by a wicked world, wicked neighbors, and perhaps (though we dread the thought) wicked family members. What has the Lord enabled us to do in our predicament?

Then why did he live in such a place where his family would be exposed to, and fall to the temptations of, the prevailing sins? We've already seen, however, that he probably didn't know how wicked this place was when he moved there. Second, the city did afford him a living, which is the same motivation for us staying where we are, although we also have to put up with things around us that aren't right. Third, he could very well have done his best, as we do, at shielding his family from his city's wickedness; don't we see this inclination of his heart in how he tried to shield his guests from the Sodomites?

Finally, this is a sobering example of what the Lord was doing in the entire story: separating out the righteous from the wicked. Not only did he separate Lot from the Sodomites, but he separated out the wicked in his family as well. You see, the Lord doesn't play favorites; just because the head of the family is righteous doesn't mean that wicked family members will be protected from God's judgment. God will expose the hearts of everyone.

- *Why did he hesitate?* Actually the translation is misleading here: the original Hebrew (and the KJV) says that he "lingered", not "hesitated." "Hesitated" sounds as if he piddled around and took his time getting ready to go, as if he didn't want to go. But it's not that he didn't want to go with the angels or didn't believe their story. Of course he believed it – that's why he pleaded with his sons-in-law to leave.

But he was wondering what to do with his family; some of them weren't coming. And he didn't realize that the disaster was waiting on *him*! The angels were under strict orders from God to hold back the disaster until Lot was safely out of range. So they were understandably urgent with him and kept trying to hurry him up. Lot, on the other hand, couldn't have known yet about the Lord's pact with Abraham, and he simply didn't know that he was the only reason Sodom still existed. This is an entirely reasonable ignorance. And if the facts were known, we might ourselves be amazed at the way God withholds his fury at our own world simply because we are still in the way. He will not strike the wicked if there is a chance that his precious children would be hurt in the process, even though it needs to be done.

- *Separating out the righteous:* Again, we have to get a hold of the point of this story. The angels came to Sodom, they found the righteous and counted heads, and determined that the city was not worth saving. So before God raised his hand in wrath to destroy them, he removed his people out of the way, so that they would not share in the punishment of the wicked. If you lose sight of this then you lose the point of the whole story.

I don't know how people can miss this. It's not as if Lot was righteous only judicially, being otherwise unrighteous in his acts. The angels were sent to find the *truly righteous* in Sodom, and Lot was the only one they found. And they determined that by watching him *in action*. The facts are there. Peter saw the point too, and he doesn't marvel at the fact that God saved a man who didn't deserve it, but that God knows how to save *his righteous ones* from the punishment due to the wicked.

- *Lot's wife:* Lot's wife is a tragic example of what often happens. If she would have continued in her husband's care, and taken advantage of her husband's faith – even though her heart led her back to Sodom – she would have been spared. But the Lord's judgment found her out and she ended up sharing the fate of the rest of the wicked. She was not a righteous one, she didn't deserve to be treated as one, and she was destroyed along with the rest. The Lord knows not only how to save the righteous from disaster, but also how to bring disaster on those trying to flee from it and use someone else's righteousness as a cover.

- *Where to go next?* There was some question as to where Lot should go next. The angels told him to flee to the hills because they had every intention of sweeping away every habitable place in the entire plain. "Don't stop anywhere in the plain! Flee to the mountains or you will be swept away!" (Genesis 19:17) But Lot didn't want to go to the mountains, probably because he was more used to living in an urban area, and he figured mountain life would be the end of him. (Genesis 19:19)

So he asked that the Lord let him stop at a town near there instead – a small one, which he figured wouldn't be any problem to the Lord. Notice that the Lord made a change of plans especially for Lot: "Very well, I will grant this request too; I will not overthrow the town you speak of." (Genesis 19:21) It seems that, if Lot hadn't gone there, it would have been destroyed too! People should have realized what an important and valuable man Lot was to have around.

Because the Lord granted his request, we must assume that it was fine to ask for it. Nobody can fault Lot for something that he asks of God, if God gives it to him. He doesn't give us things to hurt us but to help us. Again, the prayer of a righteous man is powerful and effective. (James 5:16) You can't argue with results. And the point here isn't that Lot argued with God; rather that destruction can't happen where the righteous live. The details and wording in the story point to this lesson.

- *Abraham saw the destruction:* The next morning Abraham went out and looked down at where Sodom and Gomorrah used to be, and saw the belching smoke of destruction instead. He no doubt remembered the promise that the Lord had given him, and he must have assumed the obvious: there evidently weren't even ten righteous people in Sodom. He knew his God.

And the Lord knew that Abraham was watching. (Genesis 19:29) He had already tested Abraham's faith and would test it even more with other issues. He delivered righteous Lot from the disaster, just as he promised he would. But the lesson here was that God doesn't play around: rebellious sinners would do well to take the threats of God seriously, because one day he will pour out his wrath on them, and nobody will be able to help them.

But the point about the righteous still stuck in Abraham's mind. If he knew his God as well as we might expect, he knew that his nephew was safe somewhere – the righteous *are* delivered from the punishment poured out on the wicked. We aren't told if they met up again; but it's likely that Abraham's faith in God was confirmed at some future date by hearing about Lot's miraculous escape from Sodom.

- ***The Bible's theme of deliverance:*** Please don't miss the significance of this passage of Scripture. Its point is this: *the Lord knows how to deliver his people from the wrath that comes down on the wicked.* Peter told us what to see in this story, and if we read it with that in mind (not for other issues, which complicate the point and tend to steer us off into unprofitable speculation and even wrong interpretations) then we will learn what God wants us to learn from it.

The doctrine of deliverance, or the Lord rescuing his people, is one of the major doctrines of the entire Bible. For instance, here are some of the better known rescues recorded in the Old and New Testaments:

- *the Israelites rescued from Egypt*

- *the twelve tribes rescued from their pagan neighbors through judges*

- *David rescued from King Saul*

- *Hezekiah and the Jews rescued from Sennacherib*

- *the woman caught in adultery rescued by Jesus from the Pharisees*

- *Peter rescued from prison by the angel*

- *Paul rescued from the Jews who were trying to kill him*

- *and, of course, all Christians rescued from sin and death by the blood of Christ*

If we could state the doctrine of deliverance more precisely we might say it like this: The Lord rescues, and he rescues a helpless people, from some situation which would otherwise be the end of them. Lot fits this category nicely; he therefore should take his place alongside the more famous rescues of God's people recorded in the Bible – and Peter makes sure that he does in *his* book.

The daughters' incest

The last part of Lot's story is told in Genesis 19:30-38. The gist of it is this: after fleeing from Sodom's destruction, Lot and his two daughters end up living in the mountains in a cave. The girls lost their chance to marry, so they decided that they mustn't let their father's line die with them. They took turns laying with their father (after getting him to drink wine) and both became pregnant. The two boys were named Moab and Ammon, and they became the fathers of those nations that the Bible talks about later.

This really unfortunate turn of events is probably the one thing that has convinced people today that Lot's life ended in miserable failure. But I believe that we can't draw the curtain on Lot's life until the Lord does – and as we shall see, he wasn't done with Lot yet!

- *Leaving Zoar:* We can make a guess as to why Lot left Zoar. Remember that the Lord granted Lot's request to go to Zoar instead of going to the mountains. He said then that "I will not overthrow the town you speak of." (Genesis 19:21) It seems that if Lot would not have gone there, the town of Zoar was doomed with Sodom and would also have been destroyed. While Lot was in Sodom, the Lord "cannot do anything" (Genesis 19:22); while Lot is in Zoar, that town was safe too.

But since the Lord seemed to change his mind about destroying Zoar for Lot's sake, we can suppose that the people who lived there actually deserved to be destroyed as much as the Sodomites. Probably Lot found this out after being there a short time; and after what he just saw in Sodom he probably felt that Zoar was next on the list! So he decided that perhaps the mountains weren't such a bad idea after all.

- *Living in a cave:* It seems strange to us that Lot and his daughters would live in a cave; it sounds as if they were destitute, had nothing left in life, and were only waiting for the end. But think about the situation: destitute people don't have plenty of food, nor do they have luxuries such as wine sitting around. Although he probably lost his entire business back in Sodom, he obviously found something to live on after the disaster. After all, they did continue to live after this (we're not sure where) and the daughters evidently had what they needed to raise their sons. In other words, the story doesn't tell us everything about what happened to Lot. It's only telling us the parts that pertain to the point it's making. We can't simply assume that he died penniless and forlorn. For all we know, he probably reconnected with Abraham and started life over.

- *The importance of descendants:* Since we live in an age when people are deliberately killing their offspring, it's hard to describe how important the children were to people in Bible times. Women were desperate to have children; it justified their existence in a world where possession and power and inheritance meant everything. Men wanted sons to carry on their name and honor, to work in the fields, and to keep the inheritance in the family.

The fact was, if nothing was done then Lot's name (or family, in other words) would die out immediately. It would be as if Lot had never lived, and that was unacceptable. Actually the girls were right: there probably weren't any men around who were decent enough to marry! If the Sodomites and Canaanites were representative of what kind of characters lived around there, there were no options for a husband there. Going back to Abraham's camp wouldn't help either, because Lot was a nephew of Abraham and the uncle had no more sons for Lot's daughters. He had servants, but they wouldn't have been socially acceptable for Lot's daughters (we can't forget about their culture).

So it *was* true that unless something was done, Lot's line would die out forever.

- *Drinking wine:* We mentioned before that the text doesn't say that Lot got drunk. I don't believe that this is splitting hairs, either. Other Scriptures don't hesitate to tell us if someone got drunk; if Lot did the same, I believe that it would have used the word and not spared him either. But evidently it's being very careful about how it says things, so that Peter can continue to make his claim about Lot's character, and the passage won't contain anything that obviously contradicts him.

It only says that the daughters "got him to drink wine." That can mean a whole range of things, from a little to a lot. Unfortunately many modern Christians think that drinking *any* amount of wine is getting drunk! That's simply not true; the Bible doesn't teach any such thing. The Bible does warn, however, against getting *drunk*. (For example: it may interest you to know that during Passover meal the custom was for everyone to have at least three good sized cups of wine; they were consumed at various parts of the meal, according to ceremony, and nobody got drunk from it.) At any rate, it's a mistake to focus on the wine when the passage is trying to tell us something else.

Whatever you may think about drinking wine, someone would have to prove that Lot was drunk to convict him of sin, and this passage has no proof in it. One might say, "Doesn't the fact that he didn't know what his daughters were doing prove he was drunk?" Not so: even a little alcohol will make one sleep pretty deeply the first couple of hours. But, if you think about it, the daughters probably wouldn't have achieved their goal if Lot was genuinely drunk!

- *Lot would never have done it:* One of the most important points of this passage seems to have escaped people studying this story. Unless his daughters tricked him, Lot would never have done such a thing. Awake and conscious, the thought would have been repulsive to him, since he was a *righteous ... righteous ... righteous* man.

Why do we consistently focus on Lot the sinner when it was everyone else who was sinning? Is it that Peter's enigmatic statement about his righteousness angers us and we're trying to prove otherwise? Was this ugly incident Lot's fault? He had no conscious part in it! It was foisted upon him by his daughters, completely against his wishes and without his knowledge. Was he at fault for their wickedness in any way? Couldn't he have taught them better than that? But that's the point: he probably did! If he wouldn't have done such a thing consciously, then he surely would have taught his girls better morals. Just because children turn out badly doesn't mean the parents failed. Many times that does happen; but not always. For all we know, he did his best teaching his family the fear of God. We simply have no text saying either one way or the other except the constant testimony from Peter about Lot's righteous character. Why, then, are we ready to condemn Lot for things we have no proof for?

- *Incest:* There's no question that what the girls did was detestable in God's sight. There were Laws given to Israel against this very kind of thing. It was a bad solution to a serious problem.

  You will also notice a peculiar thing about a few other Laws that Moses gave Israel. Some of them condemn the Patriarchs themselves! For example, one law (Leviticus 18:18) forbids a man to sleep with his wife's sister while still married to his wife; both, it says, must be put to death for such an abomination. The trouble is, Jacob himself did this while married to Leah – he also married her sister Rachel and had children by her too. Do we therefore shun him? Another example in Leviticus 18:9 – it says not to sleep with one's sister, even a half sister. The problem is, Abraham himself did this: he married his half-sister Sarah. Neither of these men were condemned by posterity for what they did. Not that we're making a point to ignore the Law, but in God's providence he sometimes does things in our lives that, in themselves immoral, turn out to further his purposes. So although what Lot's daughters did was wrong, the Lord certainly overruled their intentions and brought about a remarkable turn of events that he had planned for a long time.

- *Judgment:* One interesting thing about this story is that the Lord doesn't seem to be done with judging people yet. "Judgment" means to discern the truth of a matter, like a judge in a courtroom. The Lord judged Sodom, through the fact-finding mission of the angels, to be a wicked city and deserving of destruction. He uncovered the heart of Lot's wife and she fell to the same destruction as the city she loved. Now he is uncovering the hearts of Lot's daughters: children of a righteous man, they nevertheless

213

show their true colors by doing what is an abomination to the Lord. When we would think that all is well, the Lord knows better and promises to expose our hearts to the light so that all can see.

And what is more remarkable, who keeps coming out clean in spite of our most rigorous examination, in spite of the wickedness all around him, in spite of the attempts to involve him in everyone else's wickedness and punishment? This is clearly the hand of the Judge of all men, when a man survives the most determined attempts of generations of critics to ruin his character and yet not a single "fact" will stand up in court to condemn him. Instead of criticizing and kicking at Lot, we should be hoping for such a watertight testimony for ourselves – in spite of what others see in our lives to the contrary!

- **Somewhat of a miracle:** It has been noticed that it would be quite remarkable for even one of the girls to get pregnant from this single incident, since a woman has to be at a certain point in her reproductive cycle in order to conceive. For *both* of them to get pregnant is quite amazing! One wonders how much of a hand in this that God himself had, especially in light of what we will see in the next point.

- **The remarkable outcome:** This is one of those situations where a man or woman does something for one purpose and the Lord overrules for another purpose. The daughters wanted to perpetuate their father's line (a worthy enough goal) and turned to incest to do it (an unworthy means of reaching that end). The Lord also wanted to perpetuate Lot's line, but what an outcome!

Notice one of the sons – Moab. He was the father of the Moabites, who will often have dealings with Israel through the rest of the Old Testament. In fact, both nations from these two boys proved to be very troublesome for the people of God as time went on. But one exception stands out like a brilliant ray of light from Heaven: Lot was the father of Moab, and Moab was the forefather of Ruth, who was the wife of Boaz, who was the great grandfather of King David! What is even more amazing is that David is the direct ancestor of Christ – which makes Lot the *forefather of Jesus Christ!*

I'm sure that neither the daughters nor Lot realized the incredible insight behind those fateful words – " … and preserve our family line through our father." (Genesis 19:32) This situation wasn't the only time that Christ's less illustrious ancestors fell "accidentally" into the Family which brought forth the Savior. For example, there is the ugly situation between Judah and Tamar which resulted in the birth of Perez, another of Christ's ancestors. (Genesis 38) (By the way, notice how the Bible genealogies all capitalize on Christ being "of the tribe of Judah" – even in light of how it happened! This points to the fact that the Lord's eternal purposes are more important than the local circumstances. God is big enough to handle the problems involved.) But the Lord with his wisdom works wonders through unsearchable providence; what starts out as a blemish in a righteous man's life helps to bring about the greatest event in the history of mankind. Christ certainly realized his humble beginnings; but Lot would have been humbled at the thought that his own blood would run through his family's tree to eventually rise in the greatest life ever given for the sins of man.

The Modern Believer

Probably the most important reason for being careful when interpreting the story of Lot is that we must draw the correct conclusions from the story. If we assume the wrong things about Lot's character, then we are going to come up with applications of his story that the Bible doesn't want us to come up with! But if we are careful to look at it as Peter looks at it, then we will find applications in it that, surprisingly, we can use in our own lives. In fact, we have this story in order to teach us something about God that we need desperately in our age.

Wrong interpretations

First, let's look at what people usually find in this story. If you assume that Lot was a scoundrel (at worst) or a backslidden believer (at best) then you are going to come up with the following applications:

- **Stay close to God's people.** Don't do like Lot did and count fellowship with the saints something you don't need. He should have stayed close to Abraham, not gone off to live among the pagans with the excuse that he needed to improve his business. In the same way, we need to put the Church first and matters of this world second.

- **Choose Heaven's riches instead of this world's wealth.** Don't lust like Lot over the wealth and riches of this world. He saw how favorable a place the Jordan plain was to live, and with this glitter in his eyes he went off into trouble. Choose the treasures of Heaven instead and shun this world's goods.

- **Don't be friends with this world.** Certainly Lot did wrong by spending his time with the Sodomites. What fellowship has light with darkness? Even if we have to work among them, don't make friendships with the wicked that you are going to regret later.

- **Take care to train your family in the ways of the Lord.** Take a lesson from Lot's failure as a father and husband and give your family the spiritual teaching and leadership they need.

- **Get out of Sodom.** Lot should have gotten out of Sodom long before he did. Separate yourself from the world, don't live among the wicked or take part in their sinful activities. You have to get away from them before they cause you to fall asleep spiritually, and you end up caught in the same punishment they receive.

- **Don't argue with the Lord when he tells you something.** Look what happened to Lot when he argued against God's wisdom. If God tells you to go to a certain place, or do a certain thing, trust him to know what he is doing and obey him without question.

- **A life of sin will end in misery.** Old Lot paid the price for a life of rebellion and spiritual backsliding. Your sins will eventually trip you up, and you will have to pay a penalty for disobeying God's Word – even if you do find forgiveness in his grace.

All these points are valid in general, as far as they go. The problem, however, is this: does *the story of Lot* teach us these things? We can certainly find proofs from other Scriptures that these are important principles of Christian living, and we do well to teach them. But I believe that we have seen that Lot wasn't like this. We do him an injustice to accuse him of these wrongs. We are reading these sins into the story, assuming that they are there (in an effort to explain the strange events) when they really aren't.

These are not valid applications to make from the story of Lot. If you need to prove these general points, it's much easier to find someone else in the Bible as an object lesson, in light of what the passage in Peter tells us about Lot's character. If you can't see anything good in Lot then you must wait on the Lord to show you, to give you the faith you need, until he teaches you the truth about it and you finally agree with Peter's interpretation.

Besides, when we interpret the story of Lot in this way and draw these conclusions from it, we actually miss out on the real point of the story. By allowing ourselves to judge Lot and accuse him of improper behavior, we close our eyes to the truth: that this is *our* story, the application is about us in our world. We are more like Lot than we care to think, and our options are about the same as his. The question is whether we will turn out as well as he did.

An interpretation more to the point ...

Remember that the point of Peter's lesson on Lot was that the Lord knows how to rescue the righteous from the day of destruction. Now let's look at our own situation, and see if these two things are true: 1) that we live in the same predicament that Lot lived in, and 2) that we need the same salvation that Lot received from the Lord.

- *Making a living:* Although we like to think that we are so spiritual that we are doing all that we can to get ready for Heaven, in fact we spend most of our time making a nest for our (short) stay in this world. We can hardly blame Lot for looking after his business when we ourselves plan for college training, set our hopes on specific careers, move to areas where there are jobs available, buy houses in areas

218

that we like the best, involve our children in wholesome entertainment and find friends and activities for them, and many other things that make living in this world more enjoyable and comfortable.

Not that any of this is wrong; the Lord put us where we are, created us with physical needs, and made us social creatures that need interaction with others. Life is necessarily filled with concerns of this world. But if that is OK for us, why not for Lot? Was he supposed to choose a tougher place to live, a place with more hardship involved? If so, why don't we?

Some people in the past thought that if they beat their bodies and go without food and water, they would draw closer to Heaven and please God more. But the Lord enjoys blessing his people with the good things of life; there's nothing sinful about being a creature and living in this world as comfortably as possible. The sin comes in when people forget God in the midst of their good life:

> Be careful that you do not forget the LORD your God, failing to observe his commands, his laws and his decrees that I am giving you this day. Otherwise, when you eat and are satisfied, when you build fine houses and settle down, and when your herds and flocks grow large and your silver and gold increase and all you have is multiplied, then your heart will become proud and you will forget the LORD your God, who brought you out of Egypt, out of the land of slavery. (Deuteronomy 8:14)

Evidently Lot remembered the Lord and did what pleased the Lord, even while living in Sodom, taking care of his business affairs, and taking advantage of city benefits. The Lord saved him, didn't he? He promised

Abraham that he would save the *righteous*; and he rescued Lot; so we have to assume that Lot didn't forget the Lord.

We should hope to do as well – in our lives which are so full of affairs of this world and matters of comfort that too often crowd out spiritual matters.

- *Learning about the wicked:* I believe that you have found this to be true, that your neighbors turn out to be worse than you thought when you first met them. People almost never come up to you and tell you what scoundrels they really are! They try to make you think well of them from the start; if you go by first impressions, almost everyone you meet is a good person – at least by *their* standards! Most people aren't purposely trying to spread around a bad reputation of themselves.

But after a while you find yourself in a difficult situation. Their definition of what is good ends up to be quite different from yours, and you gradually find yourself at odds with them over many issues. Most of the time you don't even have the chance to talk about things with them; they simply do their wickedness and all you can do is watch in distress. They have a feeling that you don't approve, so they won't discuss it with you; but that doesn't stop them from doing it.

Isn't this usually how things go? Was it your fault that your neighbors turned out so badly? Does your presence among them change their behavior? And yet for some reason we blame Lot for not knowing the hearts of the Sodomites (something only God can know) before he moved there. Even if he had heard a rumor about their activities (which I doubt he heard much, given the circumstances of his moving around with Abraham) where would he go and not find sinners in abundance? The

Canaanites, whom Abraham lived among, were just as bad!

No, I believe that Lot innocently thought that he could live there as well as anywhere else, and he just took things as they came. I believe that the Sodomites were just as deceitful as all other wicked people are, showing a good face and defending their actions with plausible excuses. I believe that over time Lot found out that their claims didn't match with their actions, and that proved to be very distressing to him.

Our challenge is to be just as distressed with the people we have settled next to. Have our friendships compromised our firm stand on God's Word? Over time, as our friends and neighbors show their true colors, are we distressed at their filthy lives and reluctant to relate to them at all? Will our attitude toward them change – or will we want to keep the peace and give them the benefit of the doubt? If so, they are changing us to their standards (as usually happens) instead of we changing them to our standards.

- *Our witness among the wicked:* We saw that Lot had a place among the elders at the gate of the city. We didn't read how he got that place; but we mustn't slander his righteous character by assuming that he got it by going along with their wickedness. We must be ready to assume that he got it by being such a witness among them, and a help to them in their darkness, that they (reluctantly) needed him. The ways of God are life, even though the wicked hate to admit it; and they will let us help them as long as they think it serves their purposes.

The only thing that will keep our society from falling apart is our righteous lives among them. "Do everything without complaining or arguing, so that you may become blameless and pure, children of God without fault in a crooked and depraved generation, in which you shine like stars in the universe as you hold out the word of life." (Philippians 2:14-16) We have to keep telling people that there is a God, that they will be held accountable for their actions, that the wages of sin is death. We have to show them, by our own way of living, how God wants all men to be. Lot, a righteous man who was distressed by their wickedness, surely stuck out like a sore thumb among his sinful neighbors; he was no doubt the subject of ridicule and scorn as he kept himself blameless and pure among them.

That in itself is a major spiritual victory, and one that we continually fail in ourselves. If the truth were told, modern Christians are difficult to spot in our society; they fit right in with the modern way of living; they don't live by faith; they can get upset with national politics but they don't do anything to stir up the consciences of their neighbors; they are just as busy making this life more comfortable as anybody else is; although they go to church and prayer meetings, their religion doesn't change their lives to the point that their neighbors hate to be around them.

- *Leave or stay?* I find this the most incredible application that people make of Lot's story. If Lot should have left Sodom on his own, as his critics say, long before the Lord brought destruction down on the city, then the application for us also is *to leave the country we are in!* Some people do this; they wander from country to country trying to find a place where they can live to themselves and not get involved with the local affairs. But most of us don't intend to leave! We have no intention of following our advice to Lot.

222

Instead of leaving, however, we feel that it is sufficient to stay out of the affairs of the wicked. We live among them without living like them. But if this is sufficient for us, why not for Lot? If we can live in a wicked society and mourn over its wickedness, keeping ourselves as clean as possible from the filth surrounding us, then why can't we give Lot the benefit of the doubt that he could and did the same thing? In fact, this is exactly what Peter said he did! "Lot, a righteous man, who was distressed by the filthy lives of lawless men (for that righteous man, living among them day after day, was tormented in his righteous soul by the lawless deeds he saw and heard) ..." (2 Peter 2:7-8) What we hope to do, he did. We can only hope that, after living among such wickedness as our country is filled with and bombards us with daily through the media, we will still be called "righteous" as Lot was.

Besides, none of us like the thought of going off into the wilderness and living without the comforts of civilization. Pioneers have to do without electricity, cars, grocery stores, fuel oil, and all the other "necessities" of life. Very few of us could live in such conditions; we weren't raised without them and we probably wouldn't survive long without them. Yet we blame Lot for choosing a populated area, for being too soft to wander with Abraham in the wilderness!

The point, I hope you see, is that the Lord knows how to keep the righteous safe in his hands even in the middle of a difficult situation. The Lord Jesus' solution was not for everyone to leave where they live and go out somewhere in the wilderness. "My prayer is not that you take them out of the world but that you protect them from the evil one." (John 17:15) God protected Lot successfully from

223

the wickedness of Sodom; he will also protect us in our modern day Sodom. That's the point of this story.

- **The Lord's destruction:** God destroyed Sodom because of its wickedness, and we all agree with his judgment. Such a place shouldn't be allowed to exist. But (because we are often too comfortable in using double standards) we don't want God to destroy the Sodom that *we* are in! We can't imagine why he can't work with the situation and redeem our land. Hasn't he done that in the past with other wicked societies?

He has, but he doesn't owe anybody anything. He doesn't share our patriotism and he isn't obligated to keep our country on the map. He has completely destroyed other countries in past ages – not quite like Sodom was destroyed, but they are still gone nevertheless. And he could do the very same thing to us.

Now what will happen to us if he does? We don't like to think about such things, mainly because we will lose everything in the process: we could lose our money, our jobs, our homes, our families, our entertainment and hobbies, our rights, everything that we think we need to get along in life. In fact, the end could come slowly for us – we could lose these things over a long painful period of time and suffer a great deal.

People have pointed at Lot losing his entire business in the holocaust of Sodom and said, "Serves him right! He should have known better than to settle down in Sodom. Now he lost everything because he didn't obey God." But is that fair? Will we appreciate his position more if *we* lose everything because we live in this country that is so ripe for destruction? If times get harder, and it gets more difficult to feed our families, and work becomes scarce, are we going to want to hear someone blaming us for living here? Or are we going to want to hear a message of hope, that God knows how to save the righteous? Though we lose everything in this world, we know that our treasures are in Heaven; and because of that inheritance God saves us from the wrath that the rest of the hopeless world undergoes.

So the point is this: do we have an account in Heaven that shows that we are righteous in God's eyes? Will we have hope when our neighbors shoot themselves in despair? Will we weather the storm, knowing our God will preserve our lives at least, while our society struggles with sin and death? That was Lot's position, and his faith proved that he was safe spiritually though he did lose everything else. Will our faith enable us to walk away from our Sodom, our homes and businesses and pleasures, knowing that we have a better inheritance? That's going to be harder to do than you think! Jesus knew what is in our hearts; he warned us not to be like Lot's wife (he did not, you will notice, use Lot himself as the bad example!) who couldn't leave it all behind. (Luke 17:32)

- *The problems with family:* It's this part of Lot's story that makes me wonder the most if his critics are really awake. How many of us are in the same predicament! How many of our families share our spiritual concern with what is going on in our land? Who among us have our entire families dedicated to God's service? Probably very few, yet we blame Lot for not having brought his entire family around to God's ways.

We know better than this. We have probably not even tried our hardest to teach our families the fear of God, nor taken every opportunity to speak to them about eternal matters. We haven't been faithful to witness to them about

225

our God, nor have we stood solidly on God's truth when family problems come up. Yet we blame Lot for his family problems. I don't think there is a single one of us who hasn't felt the pain of not being able to get through to our families, and wondering all the time whether it was something we did wrong – or didn't do right! – that makes it so difficult for our family to see what we see.

Family is probably the most difficult group to witness to, and we all know that. Our families know us all too well; Jesus spoke the truth when he said "Only in his hometown and in his own house is a prophet without honor." (Matthew 13:57) They know that we are sinners, and our witness to them sounds more like hypocrisy than anything else. They don't see or understand that God changes people, that he re-makes them to be in the image of Christ. All they see is the same old you trying to tell them to be better people. Of course this offends them.

If our families believe the message of the Gospel it will be because of the same miracle of grace that made us believe. Imagine this: if the Lord told you that he was going to destroy your home town, and you went to your family to warn them, do you think you would get any farther than Lot did? It's doubtful! Yet the Lord *has* told us about the wrath to come on Judgment Day, and commissioned us to go out and warn sinners of its coming. We have more reason to fear this second day of wrath than ever the Sodomites did their day! But very few will listen to our message, for all that. We few who believe will barely escape with our own lives.

So perhaps Lot's family problems are more characteristic of our own family problems than we would like to admit. And perhaps we have as much hope of changing our situation as Lot did, unfortunately, because it doesn't take a love for one's family to see the truth about God, but a miracle of grace. Jesus did warn us that, far from uniting families, the Gospel is going to divide them:

Do not suppose that I have come to bring peace to the earth. I did not come to bring peace, but a sword. For I have come to turn "a man against his father, a daughter against her mother, a daughter-in-law against her mother-in-law – a man's enemies will be the members of his own household." Anyone who loves his father or mother more than me is not worthy of me; anyone who loves his son or daughter more than me is not worthy of me. (Matthew 10:34-37)

A double standard?

After thinking about the way people attack Lot, and then noticing how similar his situation is to ours, it seems to me that we've been guilty of holding to a double standard. We examine his heart and motives minutely, with a magnifying glass, assuming that he's a sinful character and attributing his troubles to his rebellion against God. We are so confident that we know what he should have done.

On the other hand, we resent anybody pointing out that we have the very same situation in our own lives. If anyone suggests that we ought to follow our own advice, we think that's ridiculous, our situation is much different, we claim. Yet the parallels are astonishing! We surely live in a modern-day Sodom, surrounded by wicked people who every day openly defy the Lord of Heaven, and our Christian witness is getting more difficult to support. We need the *same kind* of deliverance that Lot experienced. And we are hoping that, when all this is over and the Lord judges our hearts, we will also be pronounced *righteous* ... *righteous* ... *righteous* in spite of the tremendous difficulties of living in a wicked society like ours.

We wouldn't like anybody to criticize us for simply being part of this society, which some Christians from other lands often do when they come over here and watch us rich American Christians "suffer" for the cause of Christ – that is, "struggle" with 5 digit incomes, nice homes and two cars. We have bought into this system more than we are willing to admit. If we are too free in criticizing Lot for living in Sodom, then we need to put the spotlight upon ourselves for the same fault. If, on the other hand, the Lord honored Lot by preserving him in a tough environment and then delivering him from disaster – if *that* is the real point of this story – then we had better pray that the Lord is disposed to treat us with the same favor, or we will find ourselves sharing the Sodomites' fate rather than Lot's.

So in order to be fair to Lot – and to ourselves – we have to either apply to ourselves the severe standards we have burdened Lot with, or we have to give him the benefit of the doubt that he was in a predicament much as we find ourselves in. Considering what Peter has to say about the story of Lot, we would be better off taking the second approach, especially in light of the fact that we may be needing just as miraculous a rescue to get out of the way of God's wrath upon this evil generation of ours.

Conclusion

The purpose of this study wasn't to paint a picture of Lot as a perfect man, as if he were on the level of Christ! We are all sinners, and the best we can ever say is that the Lord is gracious to us and saves us from our sin. We don't want to overreact to the typical view of Lot and make him out to be better than we are.

But that's exactly the point: we want to restore his character to what Peter claims it is. He was righteous because of his faith in God; and God proved his own love and faithfulness by separating Lot out from the wicked and delivering Lot from the wrath poured out on the Sodomites. He was saved by the same process, according to the same Biblical principles, that we all are.

The story of Lot is *our* story. This is the same situation that we find ourselves in. What we need to do, when reading the story, is not to find fault with Lot, but to eagerly find out what God will do for any of his people who are in the same predicament. Out of all the characters in the Bible, Lot is one of the best models for the twentieth century man, who lives in a place much bigger than Sodom, perhaps filled with much more wickedness, and finds it increasingly difficult to live a consistent Christian testimony. We need the same God, the same mercy, the same answers, the same deliverance before we get caught up in the coming disaster. Peter got a lot of encouragement from reading the story of Lot, and we show that we understand the point of God's Word when we find hope in it too.

Notes

www.ingramcontent.com/pod-product-compliance
Lightning Source LLC
Chambersburg PA
CBHW021051090426
42738CB00006B/288